089

THIS END UP

08

PRINTED MATTER

PARIS-GONCOURT
3 · 6
1998
R. DES·GONCOURT

3.

GENERAL EDITOR:
ROGER WALTON

PRINTED MATTER

First published in 1999 by:
Hearst Books International
1350 Avenue of the Americas
New York, NY 10019
United States of America

Distributed in the United States
and Canada by:
Watson-Guptill Publications
1515 Broadway
New York, NY 10036
Telephone: (800) 451-1741;
(732) 363-4511 in NJ, AK, HI
Fax: (732) 363-0338

Distributed throughout the rest
of the world by:
Hearst Books International
1350 Avenue of the Americas
New York, NY 10019
Fax: (212) 261-6795

ISBN 0688-16938-4

First published in Europe by:
Gingko Press Verlag GmbH
Hamburger Strasse 180
D-22083 Hamburg
Germany
Telephone: (040) 291-425
Fax: (040) 291-055
email: gingko@t-online.de

ISBN 3-927258-55-5

Conceived, created and designed by:
Duncan Baird Publishers
6th Floor, Castle House
75–76 Wells Street, London W1P 3RE

Designer: Dan Sturges
Editor: Ingrid Court-Jones
Project Co-ordinator: Tara Solesbury

10 9 8 7 6 5 4 3 2 1

Typeset in Univers Condensed
Color reproduction by Colourscan, Singapore
Printed in Hong Kong

NOTE
All measurements listed in this book
are for width followed by height.

IN MEMORIAM

TIBOR KALMAN
1949–1999

FOREWORD

Printed Matter: Bound for Glory is a celebration of some of the most advanced examples of book design today. The work included displays imagination and ingenuity, process and application, analysis and inspiration.

Today, as more and more information is conveyed electronically, the days of the book might seem numbered. But even a glancing acquaintance with this collection of work will show that nothing could be further from the truth: in fact, book design is evolving healthily alongside other media. It is influenced by developments in allied fields such as screen, magazine, and commercial design and, in its turn, brings its own radical and unique contribution to other areas of graphic design.

This late-20th-century collection contains some of the most

innovative examples of contemporary book design from around

the world. The work presented here shows that a book can be

printed by hand or machine on many diverse materials; the pages

can be gathered or bound in many ways; a book can be produced

in an edition numbering from one to many thousands, and for many

different purposes. And the high quality of the pieces included

demonstrates that the book is an artifact to be admired and

cherished, as we marvel how such an object, apparently so

simple in conception, can appear in so many guises and be

adapted so cleverly to sit comfortably alongside new technology.

Printed Matter: Bound for Glory gives us a tantalizing glimpse

into the bright future of the book in the next millennium and is

essential reading for designers and book lovers everywhere.

Enjoy this book of books and celebrate the future now!

THIS END UP

INDUSTRIAL

SECTION 1

TITLE: **Fractal Building Systems**

DESIGNER/S: **Toon Stockman**

ART DIRECTOR/S: **Bernard Rommens**

DESIGN COMPANY: **Rotor**

COUNTRY OF ORIGIN: **Belgium**

PAGE DIMENSIONS: **240 x 160 mm, 9 x 6⅜ in**

WORK DESCRIPTION: **Catalog promoting aluminium building components for use in displays, exhibition stands, and interior design.**

UP

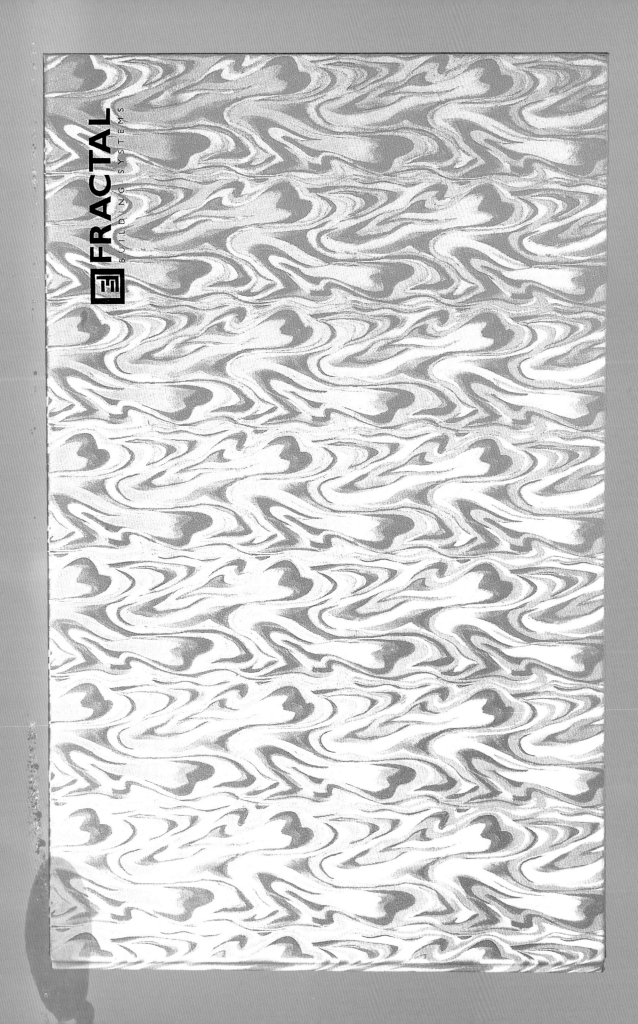

13

TITLE: : transmission 01
DESIGNER/S: Jackson Tan, Alvin Tan, Melvin Chee,
                     William Chan, Perry Neo
DESIGN COMPANY: :phunk
COUNTRY OF ORIGIN: Singapore
PAGE DIMENSIONS: 115 x 150 mm, 4$\frac{1}{2}$ x 5$\frac{7}{8}$ in
WORK DESCRIPTION: First in a series of self-promotional
'zines. It introduces the company to
potential clients and also gives an
insight into their design philosophy.
Published in a limited edition of 500,
the 'zine is accordian-folded and
perforated. It has two alternative
covers and comes packed in an
industrial bubble bag.

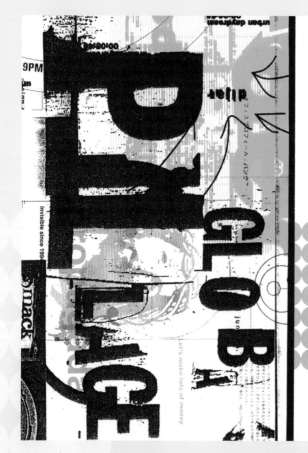

It's a Sound

Experimental procedures in hi-fidelity for visual and sound

Getting rid of background noise

One of the drawbacks of sound reproduction on tape
is the background hiss that results from the magnetic
action, which becomes most noticeable during quiet
passages. To combat hiss, a noise reduction system
known as Dolby (after R.M. Dolby, its American inventor)
is widely used.

DOLBY B NR   FOR PLAYBACK ONLY

diagnosed for: mass confusion within the perception of violence in design

symptoms: uncontrollably fierce and dangerous

prescription: 1 instinctindesignacid, 3 anti-generalizationofdesign

Instructions for use: 1. clean and dry design area to be treated. 2. apply a thin film of typo treatment to the affected area. use sparingly, avoiding eyes and mouth. if typo accidently enters eyes, rinse thoroughly. 3.use a clean dry cloth to touch up dirty areas. make sure layout is precise to recover quickly.

for external use only.
avoid contact with eyes.
store at controlled
room temperature
15°C - 30°C (59° - 86° F)

keep out of reach of children

reg. no. VIN9 597 9374

reg. no. WIL9 261 2952

reg. no. JAC9 261 2951

reg. no. PER9 510 1549

reg. no. MEL9 303 5952

reg. no. SYL9 258 3824

EAR PROTECTION REQUIRED IN THIS AREA

space

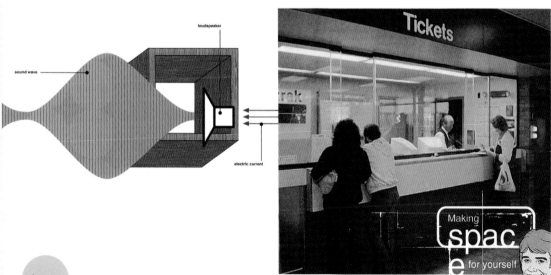

Tickets

Making
space
for yourself

loudspeaker

sound wave

electric current

Emerging sound

When the varying electric current is amplified and fed to a speaker, it is changed to sound waves that reproduce the recording.

15

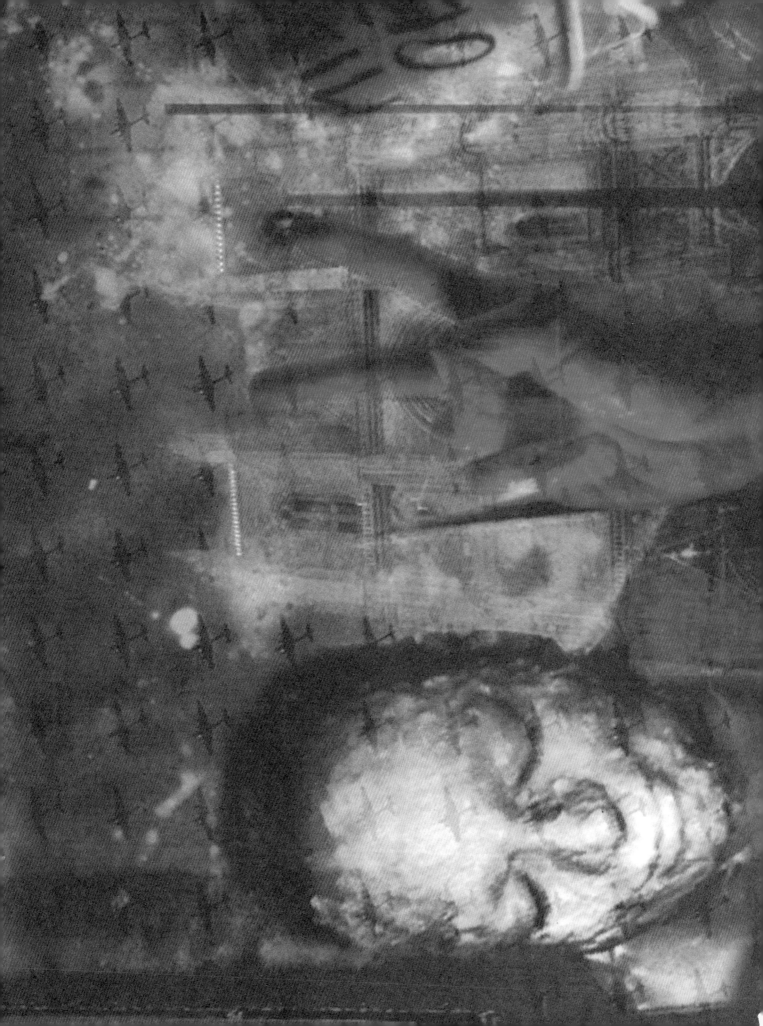

give me hot dogs and quick sex

LIBERATION
NAUGHTY
MISBEHAVIOUR
0121

693 - 5424

you mean nothing to me !

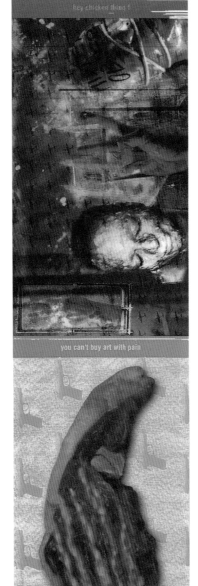

hey chicken thing !

you can't buy art with pain

Low Art Thrill

track one. sound of hurt
track two. low rent lovers
track three. hitomi
track four. upside down
track five. baby's on fire
track six. she'll kill you
track seven. european sons
track eight. cheap
track nine. glassy
track ten. television
track eleven. junkdaw saw

TITLE: Low Art Thrill

DESIGNER/S: Fluic

DESIGN COMPANY: Fluid

COUNTRY OF ORIGIN: UK

PAGE DIMENSIONS: 240 x 120 mm, 9½ x 4¾ in

WORK DESCRIPTION

Publicity kit consisting of a plastic
wallet, CD, and CD booklet to promote
the first album by the band Low Art Thrill.

STUDIO UP ONLY

THE FIRST LOW ART THRILL ALBUM
Low Art Thrill
FRVCD 1001 / 624 375-2

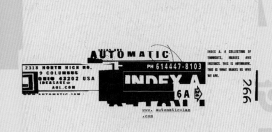

TITLE: Index A
DESIGNER/S: Charles Wilkin
ILLUSTRATOR/S: Charles Wilkin
DESIGN COMPANY: Automatic Art and Design
COUNTRY OF ORIGIN: USA
PAGE DIMENSIONS: 140 x 146 mm, 5^1/$_2$ x 5^3/$_4$ in
WORK DESCRIPTION: Self-promotional cards

BOUND FOR GLORY

A. A CATAOG OF INMOR
EMOTIONS,
XPERIENCES. THIS IS
TIC. THIS IS
IS WHO WE ARE

INDEX A. A COLLECTION OF
THOUGHTS, IMAGES AND
INSTINCT. THIS IS AUTOMATIC.
THIS IS WHAT MAKES US WHO
WE ARE.

IDEAS ARE
AUTOMATIC
PH 614447-8103
INDEX A
2318 NORTH HIGH NO.
9 COLUMBUS
OHIO 43202 USA
IDEASARE@
AOL.COM
W AUTOMATIC.IAM
6A 24
266

266

INDEX A. A COLLECTING OF THOUGHTS, IMAGES AND INSTINCT. THIS IS AUTOMATIC. THIS IS WHAT MAKES US WHAT WE ARE.

wed 5

You can't live on amusement.

PH 614447-8103

AUTOMATIC
2318 NORTH HIGH No.
9 COLUMBUS
OHIO 43202 USA
IDEASARE@
AOL.COM
WWW.AUTOMATIC-IAM

bio-box illustration

INDEX A
6A 24

IDEAS RE
AUTO M
2318 NORTH HIGH No.
9 COLUMBUS
OHIO 43202 USA
IDEASARE@
AOL.COM
WWW.AUTOMATIC-IAM

266

INDEX A. A COLLECTING OF THOUGHTS, IMAGES AND INSTINCT. THIS IS AUTOMATIC. THIS IS WHAT MAKES US WHAT WE ARE.

LIMITED TOO

PH 614447-8103

AUTOMATIC
2318 NORTH HIGH No.
9 COLUMBUS
OHIO 43202 USA
IDEASARE@
AOL.COM
WWW.AUTOMATIC-IAM

limited too packaging

INDEX A
6A 24

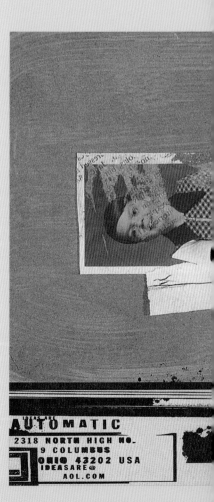

AUTOMATIC
2318 NORTH HIGH No.
9 COLUMBUS
OHIO 43202 USA
IDEASARE@
AOL.COM

TIC

PH 614447-8103

DEX A

6A 24

INDEX A. A PROCESS OF ASSEM
BLY. AN INFORMAL CONNECTING
OF ART AND HUMAN NATURE.
THIS IS AUTOMATIC. THIS IS
WHAT MAKES US WHO WE ARE.

266

ogo for
e photo

arts

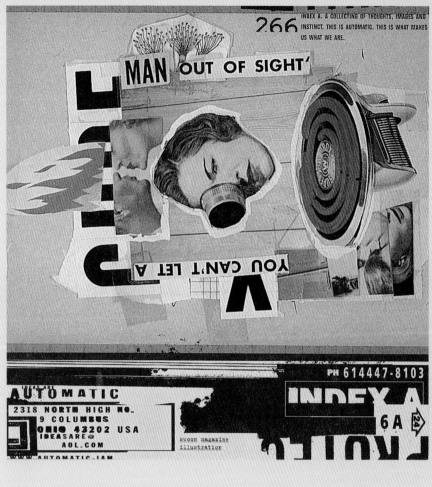

266

INDEX A. A COLLECTING OF THOUGHTS, IMAGES AND
INSTINCT. THIS IS AUTOMATIC. THIS IS WHAT MAKES
US WHAT WE ARE.

MAN OUT OF SIGHT'

YOU CAN'T LET A

PH 614447-8103

AUTOMATIC
2318 NORTH HIGH NO.
9 COLUMBUS
OHIO 43202 USA
IDEASARE@
AOL.COM
WWW.AUTOMATIC.JAM

INDEX A

6A 24

swoon magazine
illustration

266

INDEX A. A CATALOG OF INFORMATION, EMOTIONS AND
EXPERIENCES. THIS IS AUTOMATIC. THIS IS WHAT
MAKES US WHO WE ARE.

FOLLOW INSTRUCTIONS

491

PH 614447-8103

INDEX A

6A 24

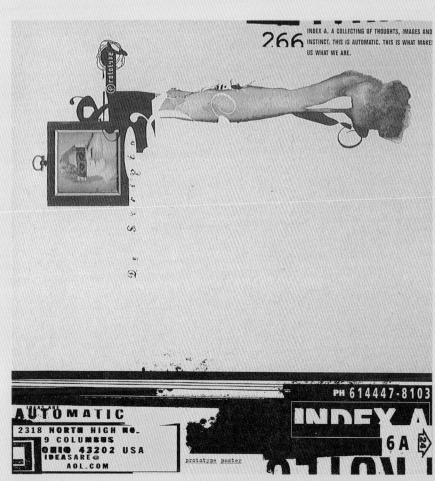

266

INDEX A. A COLLECTING OF THOUGHTS, IMAGES AND
INSTINCT. THIS IS AUTOMATIC. THIS IS WHAT MAKES
US WHAT WE ARE.

PH 614447-8103

AUTOMATIC
2318 NORTH HIGH NO.
9 COLUMBUS
OHIO 43202 USA
IDEASARE@
AOL.COM

INDEX A

6A 24

prototype poster

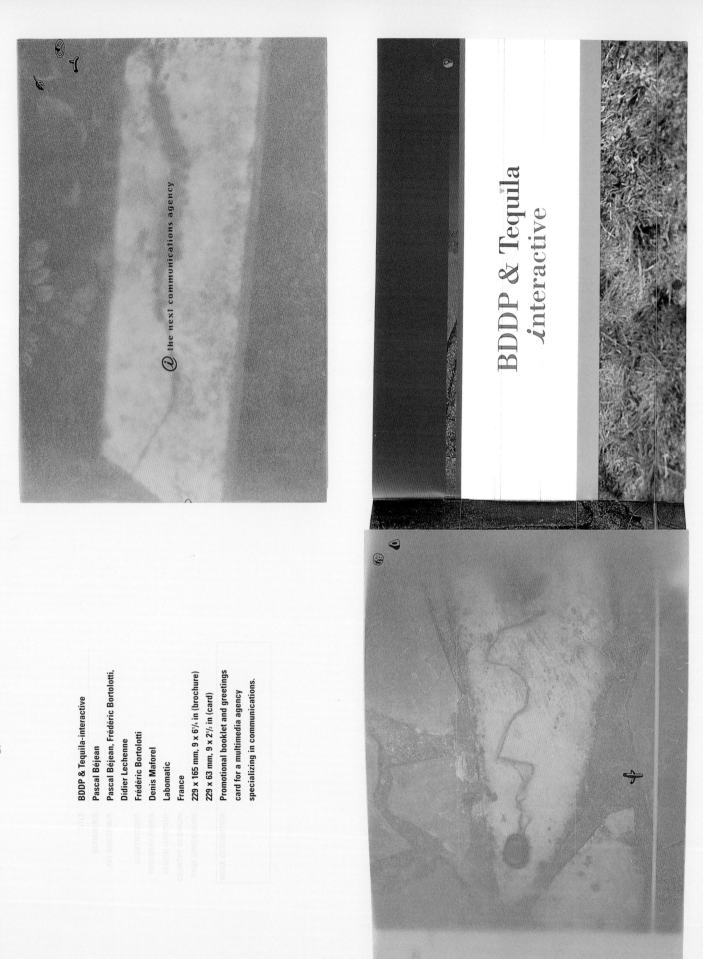

BDDP & Tequila
interactive

@ the next communications agency

TITLE	BDDP & Tequila-interactive
DESIGNERS	Pascal Béjean
ART DIRECTORS	Pascal Béjean, Frédéric Bortolotti, Didier Lechenne
ILLUSTRATORS	Frédéric Bortolotti
PHOTOGRAPHERS	Denis Maforel
DESIGN COMPANY	Labomatic
COUNTRY OF ORIGIN	France
PAGE DIMENSIONS	229 x 165 mm, 9 x 6¹/₄ in (brochure) 229 x 63 mm, 9 x 2¹/₂ in (card)
WORK DESCRIPTION	Promotional booklet and greetings card for a multimedia agency specializing in communications.

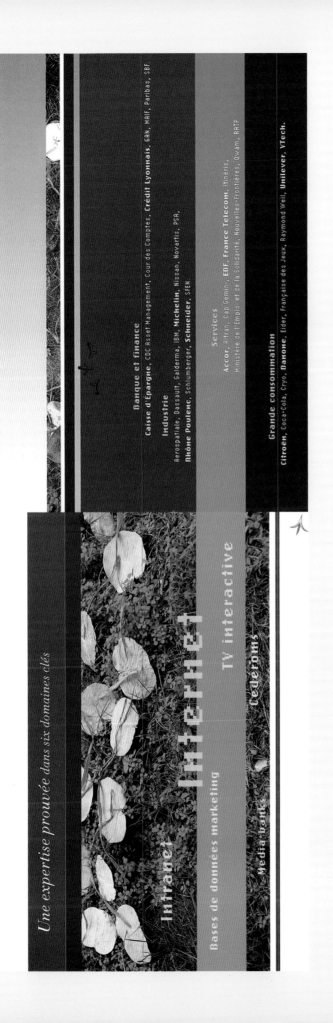

Une expertise prouvée dans six domaines clés

Intranet

Internet

TV interactive

Bases de données marketing

Cederoms

Media banks

Banque et finance
Caisse d'Epargne, CDC Asset Management, Cour des Comptes, **Crédit Lyonnais**, GAN, MAIF, Paribas, SBF.

Industrie
Aerospatiale, Dassault, Galderma, IBM, **Michelin**, Nissan, Novartis, PSA,
Rhône Poulenc, Schlumberger, **Schneider**, SFIM.

Services
Accor, Bitran, Cap Gemini, **EDF**, France Telecom, Itineris,
Ministère de l'Emploi et de la Solidarité, Nouvelles-Frontières, Qwam, RATP.

Grande consommation
Citroën, Coca-Cola, Cryo, **Danone**, Elder, Française des Jeux, Raymond Weil, **Unilever**, VTech.

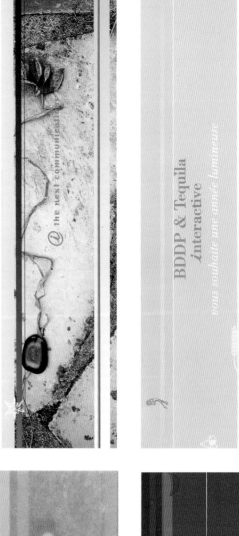

@ the next communicati

BDDP & Tequila
Interactive
vous souhaite une année lumineuse

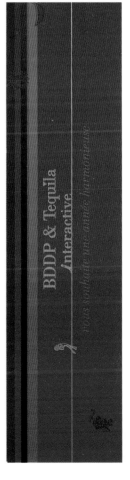

Belle année 1999.

BDDP & Tequila
Interactive
vous souhaite une année harmonieuse

hi

,this is me, i'm a bag

. like you i'm unique, and like you, i have my dreams, my aspirations and my bad days. **i'd like to give you a glimpse into bag life,** i'd also like to introduce you to our Maker. we think He's special but He wouldn't dream of talking about himself so i'll do it for Him. He cares for us and does His absolute best to send us out into the world totally prepared for our tasks. He thinks that's only as it should be so what is there to talk about.?

our mission as you know is to transport precious merchandise and for this task our Maker endows us with strength both **physical and spiritual.** we are also compassionate and caring and comport ourselves in a confident not to mention stylish manner because we are to be ambassadors for the creme de la creme of the fashion and design world.

we are lovingly created and nurtured in mills in hong kong and china from deluxe papers. the most exquisite ,exclusive and complex papers in the world. from conception to birth, when he imbues each of us with our individual identities, He lovingly prepares us for our mission.

together with our robust bag cousins of the polythene persuasion and our rigid relatives the packaging people we are groomed for our part in the vast scheme of life. when our Maker deems ready we are swiftly and efficiently dispatched from a vast global network of manufacturing and distribution facilities to whatever location has been assigned to us.

finally we can fulfil our purpose. realise our destiny. i feel blessed because i know our Maker watches over us every instant of our lives.

i've enjoyed talking to you and look forward to doing so again soon. in the meantime may i with all humility ask that when you meet up with me or my relatives would you please be thoughtful and>>

>>handle us kindly we have feelings too,

just like you<<

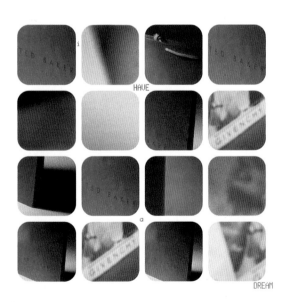

i HAVE a DREAM

FILL ME UP. FILL ME

fill me up

HOLD ME

HOLD ME

CONTAIN LOVE
DREAM FILL
ABUSE PICKUP
DISCARD USE
LIBERATE

TITLE:	Me Book
DESIGNER/S:	Nitesh Mody, Alan Carruthers,
	Ken Clarke
ART DIRECTOR/S:	Nitesh Mody, Alan Carruthers
PHOTOGRAPHER/S:	Alan Carruthers
DESIGN COMPANY:	MOOT
COUNTRY OF ORIGIN:	UK
PAGE DIMENSIONS:	210 x 210 mm, 8¼ x 8¼ in

Here, and previous spread

WORK DESCRIPTION:
Promotional brochure, box, and audio tape produced for
Keenpac UK, a manufacturer of quality carrier bags and
packaging for high-profile fashion retailers and designers.

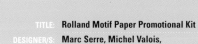

TITLE: **Rolland Motif Paper Promotional Kit**

DESIGNER/S: **Marc Serre, Michel Valois,**
Christine Côté

ART DIRECTOR/S: **Marc Serre, Daniel Fortin,**
George Fok

ILLUSTRATOR/S: **Marc Serre**

PHOTOGRAPHER/S: **Dennis Kunkel, John Tsukano**

DESIGN COMPANY: **Époxy**

COUNTRY OF ORIGIN: **Canada**

PAGE DIMENSIONS: **279 x 432 mm, 11 x 17 in**

WORK DESCRIPTION:

This book of paper samples introduces an innovative
range of papers featuring lines, curves, and screens
that are watermarked into, not printed onto, the paper.
Subtle details, such as organic motifs based on
microscopic life, turn this apparently ordinary
paper into something extraordinary.

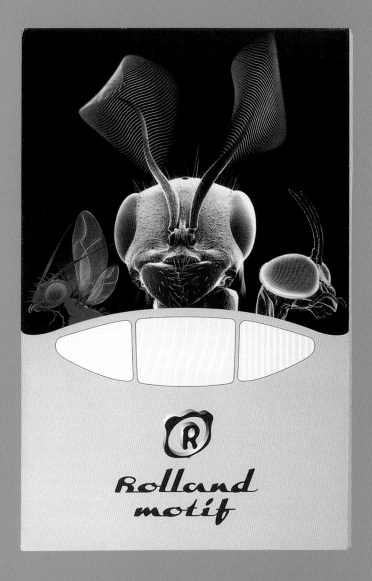

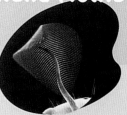

See the **Screen** motif
on the termite's wings?
You're cleared for takeoff.

Vous apercevez
le motif **Tamis**
sur les ailes du termite?
Prêt pour le décollage!

The 3 Rolland Motifs

Observe the **Curves** motif
on the ant's antennae?
Signal's coming in
loud and clear.

Vous remarquez
le motif **Courbes**
sur l'antenne
de la fourmi?
Un signal on ne peut
plus clair.

Trois Rolland Motif

Notice the **Lines** motif
on the praying
mantis eye?
Praise the lord.

Vous voyez
le motif **Lignes**
dans l'oeil
de la mante
religieuse?
Dieu soit béni.

Each motif
available
in Pure White,
Cream White,
Pale Brown
and Warm Green.

Chaque motif
est offert
en Blanc pur,
Blanc crème,
Brun pâle et Vert chaud.

TITLE:
DESIGNER/S:
ART DIRECTOR/S:
PHOTOGRAPHER/S:
DESIGN COMPANY:
COUNTRY OF ORIGIN:
PAGE DIMENSIONS:

All details as previous spread

WORK DESCRIPTION:

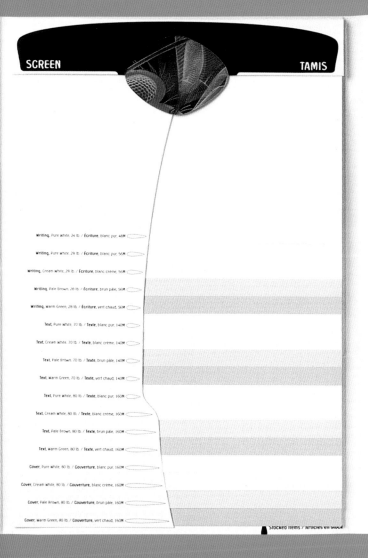

Writing, Pure white, 24 lb. / **Écriture**, blanc pur, 48M

Writing, Pure white, 28 lb. / **Écriture**, blanc pur, 56M

Writing, Cream white, 28 lb. / **Écriture**, blanc crème, 56M

Writing, Pale Brown, 28 lb. / **Écriture**, brun pâle, 56M

Writing, Warm Green, 28 lb. / **Écriture**, vert chaud, 56M

Text, Pure white, 70 lb. / **Texte**, blanc pur, 140M

Text, Cream white, 70 lb. / **Texte**, blanc crème, 140M

Text, Pale Brown, 70 lb. / **Texte**, brun pâle, 140M

Text, Warm Green, 70 lb. / **Texte**, vert chaud, 140M

Text, Pure white, 80 lb. / **Texte**, blanc pur, 160M

Text, Cream white, 80 lb. / **Texte**, blanc crème, 160M

Text, Pale Brown, 80 lb. / **Texte**, brun pâle, 160M

Text, Warm Green, 80 lb. / **Texte**, vert chaud, 160M

Cover, Pure white, 80 lb. / **Couverture**, blanc pur, 160M

Cover, Cream white, 80 lb. / **Couverture**, blanc crème, 160M

Cover, Pale Brown, 80 lb. / **Couverture**, brun pâle, 160M

Cover, Warm Green, 80 lb. / **Couverture**, vert chaud, 160M

Stocked Items / Articles en stock

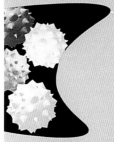

Envolez-vous

Rolland Motif vous apporte plus
de créativité, plus d'impact, plus de
distinction. Rolland Motif, c'est aussi
de superbes feuilles écriture, texte et
couverture avec motifs en filigrane –
Tamis, Courbes et Lignes. Non pas
des motifs imprimés, qui briment la
créativité. Mais de véritables filigranes,
éloquents symboles de prestige.

Métamorphose du papier. Éclat du blanc
quand vous voulez du blanc et richesse
des couleurs quand vous choisissez
la couleur. Toujours ultra lisse.
Avec 30 % de fibres postconsommation,
Rolland Motif couleurs affiche l'Éco-Logo.
Cette feuille alcaline est offerte dans les
formats et poids les plus populaires.

RENDRE L'ORDINAIRE
EXTRAORDINAIRE

Adieu
les bébites!

Rolland Motif est garanti sans problème
sur imprimante à laser. Compatible
avec toutes les imprimantes à jet d'encre,
il est aussi impeccable sur presse.
De plus, son prix se compare
avantageusement à celui
des meilleurs papiers fins
non filigranés.

Assortissez et mélangez les couleurs
pour la papeterie, les rapports annuels
et tous vos projets imprimés. Orientez
les motifs à l'horizontale ou à la
verticale. Donnez des ailes à votre
créativité. Vous aurez la piqûre.

bienvenidos

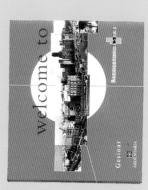

welcome to

welcome
to the centre of Spain
bienvenidos al centro de España

Gesinar

ARDUVARIA

Property Sales Pack

Jorge Garcia
Valerie de la Dehesa
Tau Diseño
Spain
310 x 314 mm, 12²/₄ x 12³/₈ in
Brochure, CD, and presentation box
to promote a prestigious property
sale in central Spain.

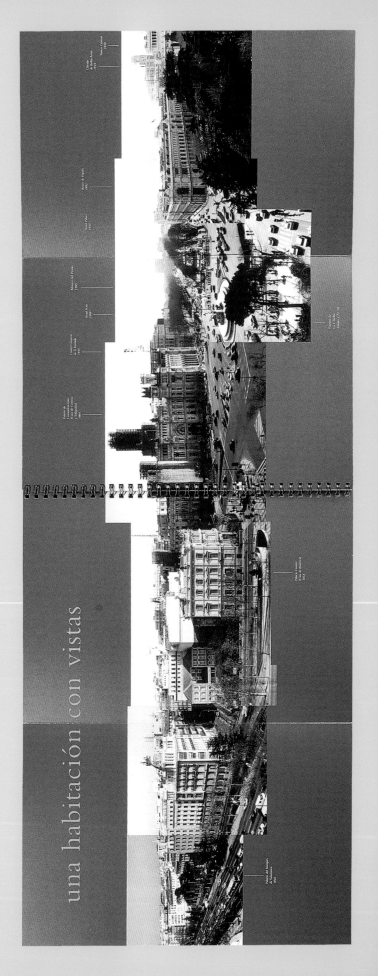

una habitación con vistas

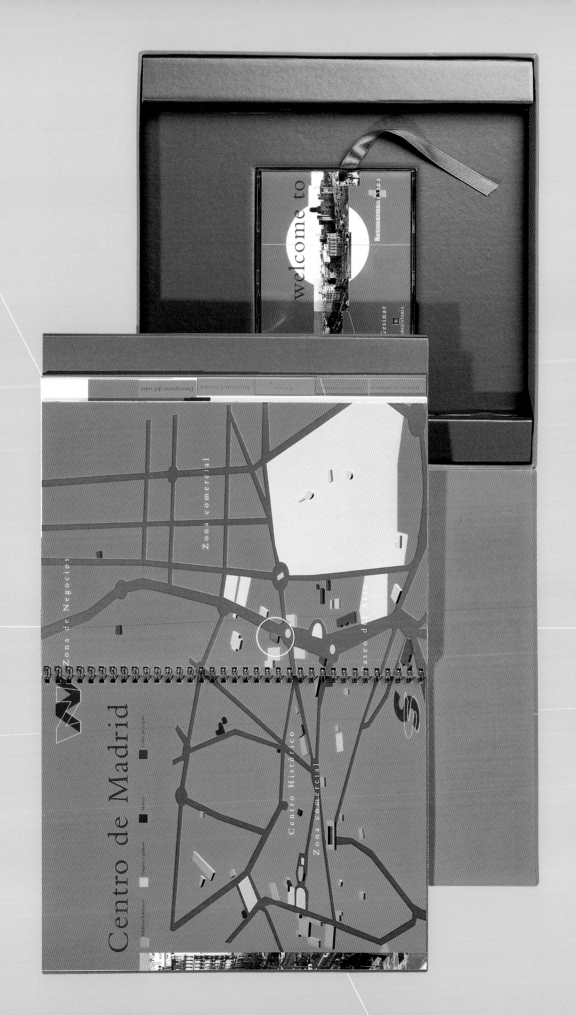

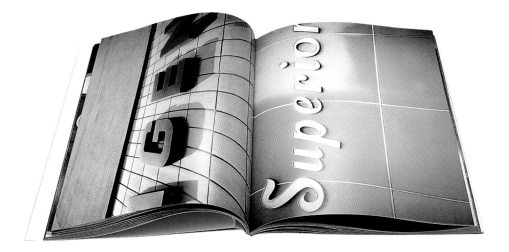

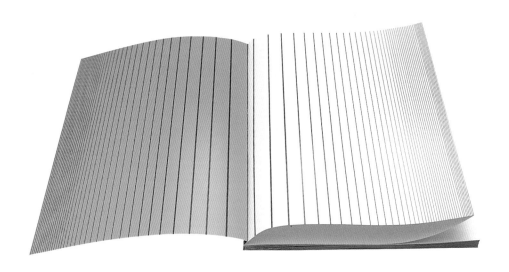

TITLE:	**Sign 2: Inspiration im Alltag**
DESIGNER/S:	**Antonia Henschel**
PHOTOGRAPHER/S:	**Antonia Henschel**
DESIGN COMPANY:	**Sign Kommunikation**
COUNTRY OF ORIGIN:	**Germany**
PAGE DIMENSIONS:	**210 x 297 mm, 8^1/$_4$ x 11^3/$_4$ in**
WORK DESCRIPTION:	**Self-promotional book**
	exploring sources of inspiration
	found in everyday life.

BOUND FOR GLORY

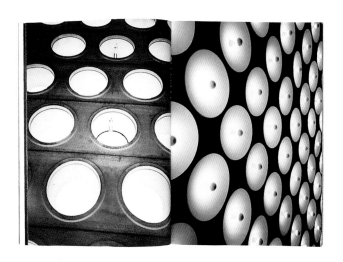

fao ROGER WALTON
DUNCAN BAIRD PUBLISHERS
6th floor
75-76 WELLS ST
LONDON
W1P 3RE

TITLE: **Red Design Promotional Booklet**
DESIGNER/S: **H. Makgill, E. Templeton**
ILLUSTRATOR/S: **Red Design**
DESIGN COMPANY: **Red Design**
COUNTRY OF ORIGIN: **UK**
PAGE DIMENSIONS: **139 x 122 mm, 5¹/₂ x 4³/₄ in**
WORK DESCRIPTION: **Self-promotional booklet that was sent to both potential and existing clients in summer 1998.**

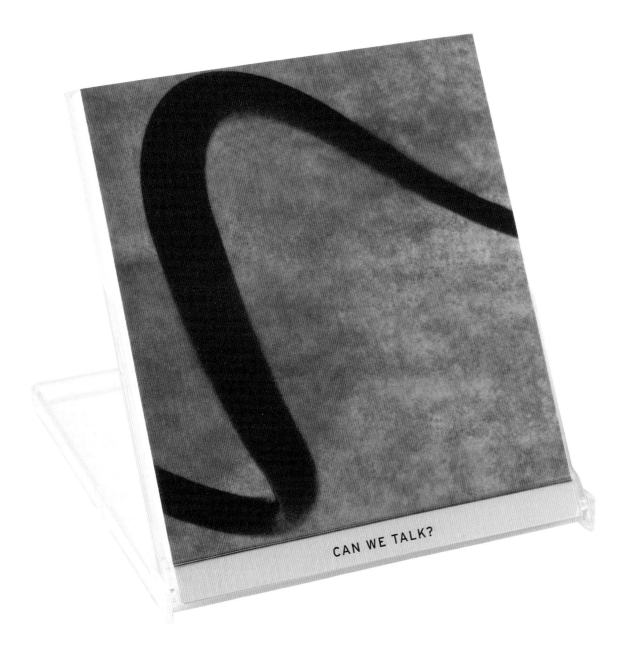

CAN WE TALK?

TITLE:	Can We Talk?
DESIGNER/S:	Carlos Segura, Sara Ploehn
ART DIRECTOR/S:	Carlos Segura
DESIGN COMPANY:	Segura Inc.
COUNTRY OF ORIGIN:	USA
PAGE DIMENSIONS:	118 x 138 mm, 4⁵/₈ x 5¹/₂ in

WORK DESCRIPTION:

Letterpress calendar promoting a stock photography book entitled *Signal*, released by picture library Tony Stone Images. The calendar illustrates the rich variety of ways in which humans communicate.

TRAVEL SYMBOLS

Baggage Check · Porter · Baggage Lockers · Baggage Claim · Unclaimed Baggage · Customs · Used Towels · Used Cups · Garbage · Women's Restroom · Men's Restroom · Washroom · Restaurant · Snack Bar · Coffee · Bar · Lost and Found · Cloakroom · Drinking Water · Safe Deposit · Fire Extinguisher · Room Service · Cleaning Service · Bellboy · Lost Child · No Entry · Parking · Escalators Up and Down · Stairs Up and Down · Elevators

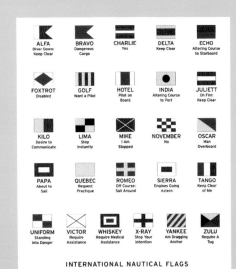

INTERNATIONAL NAUTICAL FLAGS

ALFA — Diver Down: Keep Clear · BRAVO — Dangerous Cargo · CHARLIE — Yes · DELTA — Keep Clear · ECHO — Altering Course to Starboard · FOXTROT — Disabled · GOLF — Want a Pilot · HOTEL — Pilot on Board · INDIA — Altering Course to Port · JULIETT — On Fire: Keep Clear · KILO — Desire to Communicate · LIMA — Stop Instantly · MIKE — I Am Stopped · NOVEMBER — No · OSCAR — Man Overboard · PAPA — About to Sail · QUEBEC — Request Practique · ROMEO — Off Course: Sail Around · SIERRA — Engines Going Astern · TANGO — Keep Clear of Me · UNIFORM — Standing Into Danger · VICTOR — Require Assistance · WHISKEY — Require Medical Assistance · X-RAY — Stop Your Intention · YANKEE — Am Dragging Anchor · ZULU — Require a Tug

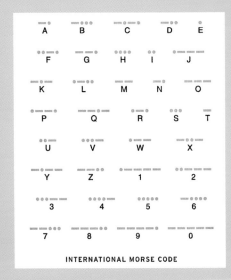

INTERNATIONAL MORSE CODE

A B C D E F G H I J K L M N O P Q R S T U V W X Y Z 1 2 3 4 5 6 7 8 9 0

HOBO SIGNS

No Use Going This Way · This Way · Hit the Road Quick! · Good Road to Follow · Road Spoiled (full of hobos) · Nothing to be Gained Here · This Is the Place · Dangerous Neighborhood · Indifferent to Hobos · Halt · You Can Camp Here · Fresh Water Safe Campsite · Dangerous Water · All Right · Good Place for a Handout · Ill-Tempered Man Lives Here · Well-Guarded House · These People Are Rich · Kind Lady Lives Here · Food Here if You Work · Kind Woman Tell Sad Story · Religious Talk Gets Free Meal · Will Care for Sick · Doctor Here No Charge · Free Telephone · Alcohol in This Town · You Can Sleep in Hayloft · Keep Quiet · Hold Your Tongue · Easy Mark, Sucker · Barking Dog Here · Vicious Dog Here · Trolley Stop · Good Place to Catch Train · Not a Safe Place · Man with Gun Lives Here · Prepare to Defend Self · Dishonest Person Lives Here · Cowards: Will Give To Get Rid of You · You'll Be Cursed Out · You'll Get a Beating Here · Police Here Frown on Hobos · Alert Authorities Here · There Are Thieves About · Crime Committed · Courthouse; Precinct Station · Law Officer Lives Here

SEMAPHORE FLAG SIGNALS

A and 1 · B and 2 · C and 3 · D and 4 · E and 5 · F and 6 · G and 7 · H and 8 · I and 9 · J and 'alphabetic' · K and zero · L · M · N · O · P · Q · R · S · T · U · V · W · X · Y · Z · Numerical sign · Annual Sign · Error

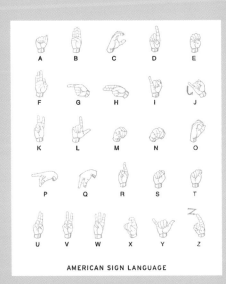

AMERICAN SIGN LANGUAGE

A B C D E F G H I J K L M N O P Q R S T U V W X Y Z

JULY

S	M	T	W	T	F	S
				1	2	3
4	5	6	7	8	9	10
11	12	13	14	15	16	17
18	19	20	21	22	23	24
25	26	27	28	29	30	31

CB RADIO TEN CODES

Code	Meaning	Code	Meaning
10-1	Receiving poorly	10-36	Correct time is ____
10-2	Receiving well	10-37	Wrecker needed at ____
10-3	Stop transmitting	10-38	Ambulance needed at ____
10-4	Message received	10-39	Your message delivered
10-5	Relay message to ____	10-41	Please turn to channel ____
10-6	Busy, please stand by	10-42	Traffic accident at ____
10-7	Out of service	10-43	Traffic tie up at ____
10-8	In service, subject to call	10-44	I have a message for you
10-9	Repeat message	10-45	All units within range please report
10-10	Transmission completed	10-50	Break channel
10-11	Talking too rapidly	10-60	What is next message number?
10-12	Visitors present	10-62	Unable to copy, use phone
10-13	Advise weather/road conditions	10-63	Net directed to ____
10-16	Make pickup at ____	10-64	Net clear
10-17	Urgent business	10-65	Awaiting your next message
10-18	Anything for us?	10-67	All units comply
10-19	Nothing for you, return to base	10-70	Fire at ____
10-20	My location is ____	10-71	Proceed with transmission in sequence
10-21	Call by telephone		
10-22	Report in person to ____	10-77	Negative contact
10-23	Stand by	10-81	Reserve hotel room for ____
10-24	Completed last assignment	10-82	Reserve room for ____
10-25	Can you contact ____	10-84	My telephone number is ____
10-26	Disregard last information	10-85	My address is ____
10-27	I am moving to channel ____	10-91	Talk closer to mike
10-28	Identify your station	10-93	Check my frequency on this channel
10-29	Time is up for contact		
10-30	Does not conform to FCC rules	10-94	Please give me a long count
10-32	I will give you a radio check	10-99	Mission completed, all units secure
10-33	Emergency traffic	10-200	Police needed at ____
10-34	Trouble at this station		
10-35	Confidential information		

SEPTEMBER

S	M	T	W	T	F	S
			1	2	3	4
5	6	7	8	9	10	11
12	13	14	15	16	17	18
19	20	21	22	23	24	25
26	27	28	29	30		

03 CD VERSO

Il arrivait à toucher un public plus vaste, ceux qui serraient,
ceux qui était incapables de serrer, mais qui tous allongeaient leur fric.

04 AFFICHE

Puisque toutes ces royalties remplissaient le réservoir de la Triumph
et l'habillaient, lui, de complets J. Press, McClintic ne pouvait

bienflétés bléssers n'ski de 60s

FEAT :
AMBITRONIQUES /STEVE ARGÜELLES BENOÎT DELBECQ/
+ REQ
+ DR. BONE / ezten /

PIANO .PREPARE .SAMPLER
SYNTHETISEURS .BATTERIE /
PLATINES .PLATINES
EFFETS ELECTRONIQUES

FOU FREESTYLERS fréquences

JEUDI 1ER ET VENDREDI 2 AVRIL 1999

AUBERVILLIERS
LES LABORATOIRES D'AUBERVILLIERS
41 RUE LECUYER, 20H30
80F-50F (TARIF REDUIT)
ACCES : ROUTE DE LA VILLETTE,
A4 : JEAN JAURES
METRO AUBERVILLIERS-PANTIN - 4 CHEMINS (L.7)
BILLETS BANLIEUES BLEUES 01 4922 1010
OU FNAC, VIRGIN, EXTRAPOLE ETC.

TITLE:	**Labomatic**
DESIGNER/S:	**Labomatic**
ILLUSTRATOR/S:	**Labomatic**
DESIGN COMPANY:	**Labomatic**
PHOTOGRAPHER/S:	**Labomatic**

COUNTRY OF ORIGIN:	**France**
PAGE DIMENSIONS:	**234 x 164 mm, 9¹/₄ x 6¹/₂ in**
WORK DESCRIPTION:	**Self-promotional brochure focusing on design for the music industry.**

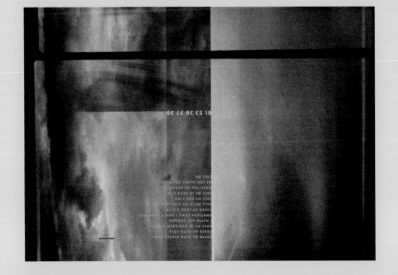

Cette conversation fut à l'origine de ce Set 'Reset
qui était en passe de devenir l'indicatif de la formation.

Le technicien de son, en effet, avait révélé à McClintic
l'existence d'un double circuit à trois électrodes, appelé flip-flap.

TELE TRAVAIL.

SANS PRACTICAL SIZE.CEDRIC PIGOT.ERIK MINKKINEN. FRAGILE.CLIC..EVA REVOX.GROUP+GRIS
ULTRA MILKMAUDE.CHRISTIAN BOUTJOU.COMMANDO.COM.OSAKA BONDAGE.ETRE VINCENT'S FACE.

live (21:30→00:00):
GENERAL MAGIC+PITA
CHRISTIAN FENNESZ

visuels:
TINA FRANK/SKOT

mx (00:00→06:00):
MEGO+BURO

9:50 65.0

buro 8:
MEGO NIGHT
FEVER

mercredi
24 FEV 1999
A L'EVASION
26 bd de bonne-nouvelle
paris10e
(m° bonne nouvelle) 60f

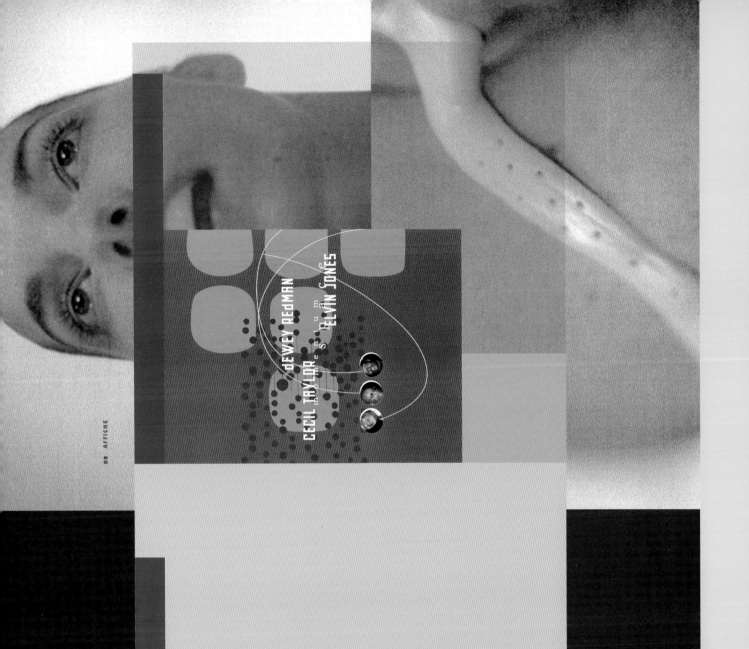

CECIL TAYLOR m e n t u m s
dEWEY REDMAN
ELVIN JONES

Flap-Flip, autrefois j'étais hip, Flip-Flap, me voilà dans la vape.
Set/Reset ...

lieu ouvert
du mardi 17 au dimanche 22 nov.

37 rue de charonne paris11, m°bastille ou ledru-rollin ou voltaire, au fond de la cour à droite

EXPOSITION akïko
zabou m.
belgique

MARDI 17 NOVEMBRE
VERNISSAGE à partir de 18h

CONCERT à 20h
cédric pigot

DIMANCHE 22 NOVEMBRE

concert: clic.
+ open biro...

TITLE: *In* Limited Edition Book

DESIGNER/S: Tamar Cohen, David Slatoff

DESIGN COMPANY: Slatoff & Cohen Partners Inc.

COUNTRY OF ORIGIN: USA

PAGE DIMENSIONS: 245 x 260 mm, 9¾ x 10¼ in

WORK DESCRIPTION:

Book devised for the production company Radical Media to present a magazine-format TV show called *In*. The book contains many pockets and envelopes to create an interactive experience for the reader.

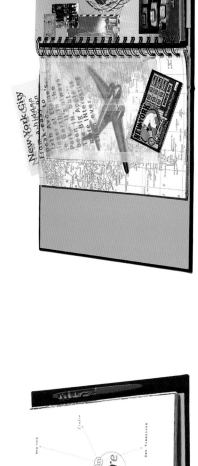

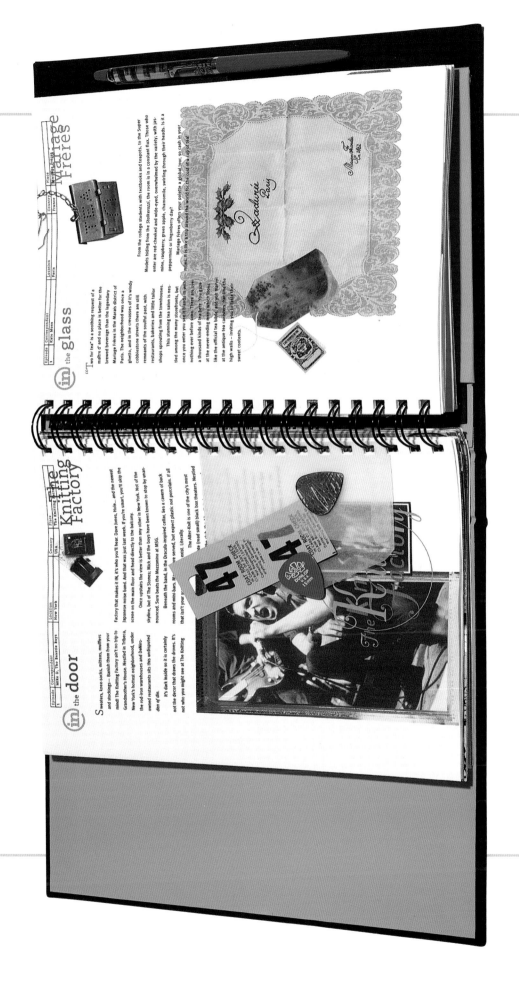

Mariage Frères

Episode	Correspondent	Place	Country	Location
1	Kate Moss	Mariage Frères	France	Paris

in the glass

"Two for tea" is a soothing request of a maître d' and no place is better for the brewed beverage than the legendary Mariage Frères in the Marais district of Paris. The neighborhood was once a ghetto, and in the crevasses of it's windy cobblestone streets there are still remnants of the soulful past, with restaurants, bakeries and little tailor shops sprouting from the townhouses.

This stunning tea salon is nestled among the many storefronts, but once you enter you see the birds in with nothing ever before seen. There are over a thousand kinds of tea here. You gaze at the never-ending menu which boasts like the official tea bible. And yet marvel at the antique tea canisters that line the high walls — inviting you to taste their sweet contents.

From the college students with textbooks and teapots, to the Super Models fleling from the Stoltenazzi, the room is in a constant flux. Those who enter are red-cheeked and wide-eyed, overwhelmed by the variety; with jasmine, raspberry, green apple, chamomile, swirling through their heads. Is it a peppermint or lingonberry day?

Mariage Frères offers your palette a global tour, so cash in your miles. It is like a trip around the world for the cost of a cup of tea.

The Knitting Factory

Episode	Correspondent	Place	Country	Location
1	Mike D, The Beastie Boys	The Knitting Factory	USA	New York

in the door

Sweaters, knee-socks, mittens, mufflers and stockings— Banish them from your mind! The Knitting Factory ain't no trip to Grandmother's House. Nestled in TriBeCa, New York's hottest neighborhood, under the rod-iron warehouses and DeNiro-owned restaurants sits this undisputed den of din.

It's dark inside so it is certainly not the decor that draws the droves. It's not who you might see at The Knitting Factory that makes it IK, it's who you'll hear. Dave Jones, Hole... and the newest Japanese noise band. And that was just last week. If you're smart, you'll skip the scene on the main floor and head directly to the balcony.

Once upstairs the view is better than any other in New York. Not of the skyline, but of The Stones; Mick and the boys have been known to stop by unannounced. Sure beats the Mezzanine at MSG.

Beneath the band, in the Dracula-inspired cellar, lies a cavern of back rooms and mini-bars. Martinis are served, but expect plastic not porcelain. If all that isn't your scene...

The Alter-Knit is one of the city's most intimate (read small) black box theaters. Nestled...

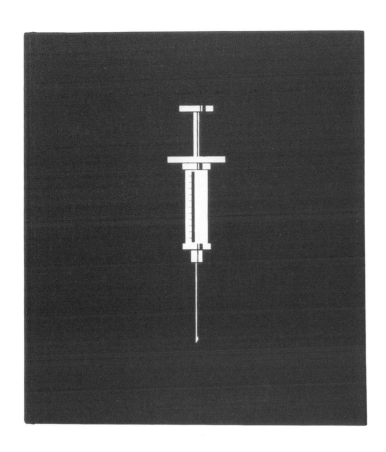

TITLE	**Modular New Items**
DESIGNER	**Bernard Rommens**
ART DIRECTOR	**Bernard Rommens, Toon Stockman**
PHOTOGRAPHER	**Patrick Hanssens**
DESIGN COMPANY	**Rotor**
COUNTRY OF ORIGIN	**Belgium**
PAGE DIMENSIONS	**245 x 280 mm, 9³/₄ x 11 in**
WORK DESCRIPTION	**Catalog featuring all the latest lines from a contemporary lighting company.**

TITLE: [T-26] Box Set
DESIGNER/S: Carlos Segura, Susana Detembleque
ART DIRECTOR/S: Carlos Segura
DESIGN COMPANY: Segura Inc.
COUNTRY OF ORIGIN: USA
PAGE DIMENSIONS: 317 x 457 mm, 12¹/₄ x 18 in
WORK DESCRIPTION: Broadsheets featuring and promoting the Type Foundry's T-26 typefaces. They form part of a limited edition box set of promotional materials for these fonts.

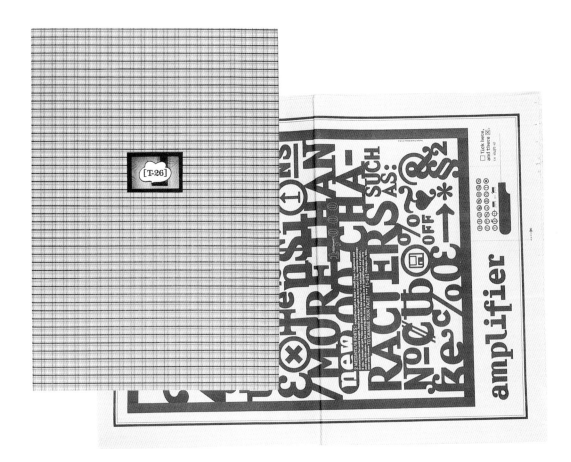

CUTTING ROOMS
PROFESSIONAL IN HOUSE RECORDING FACILITY CONSISTENT WITH INDUSTRY technology WITH CONSTANT UPGRADING AVAILABLE AS PART OF MUSIC COURSES, BUT ALSO FOR external hire.

(*FFWD)

KIT .... NICE SOFT CHAIRS, SWIVEL STICKS, KNOBBLY BUTTONS THAT LIGHT UP, OH, AND £1/4M OF THE LATEST TECHNOLOGY, BASED IN 3 STUDIOS INCLUDING FULLY AUTOMATED DESKS AND DIGITAL 16 AND 24 TRACK.

Site   ABRAHAM MOSS
Bands: JAMES OASIS
              PURESSENCE

Clients: Virgin, Polygram, Warner Chappell
Corporate: BBC, Granada Television

ROUND AND ROUND AND ROUND AND ROUND AND ROUND
Paul o'Brien or Mike Baker on
+44 (0)161 740 9438

MUSIC AND NEW MEDIA MANAGEMENT

IS A MANAGEMENT RESOURCE CONSISTING OF PROMOTERS, MANAGERS, MUSICIANS AND DJ'S. THE FUTURE OF THE LABEL AND CONFERENCE ARM IS IN THE HANDS OF THIS DYNAMIC NEW TALENT, WHO ARE REINFORCING THEIR SKILLS BY SIMULTANEOUSLY STUDYING A TWO YEAR PROFESSIONAL HND QUALIFICATION.

THE DEVELOPMENT PROGRAMME INCLUDES ADMINISTRATION, NEW MEDIA PRODUCTION, AV PRODUCTION, PROJECT MANAGEMENT, MARKETING & COMMUNICATIONS, BUSINESS AFFAIRS, LANGUAGES, INTERNATIONAL STUDIES AND INCLUDES INDUSTRY VISITS, GUEST SPEAKERS AND EVENTS SUCH AS THE 1999 MIDEM CONFERENCE AND TRADE EVENT IN CANNES.

THE MANAGEMENT TEAM ARE BASED AT ARDEN IN A FULLY EQUIPPED OFFICE ENVIRONMENT. EVERY TEAM MEMBER IS INVOLVED NOT JUST IN THE DEVELOPMENT OF THE RAW FISH LABEL, BUT THEIR OWN BUSINESS PROJECTS WHICH INCLUDE ARTIST REPRESENTATION, NEW MEDIA PROJECT MANAGEMENT, CLUB PROMOTION AND LABEL MARKETING.

THIS SYSTEM WILL TRAIN A WHOLE NEW BREED OF CREATIVE MANAGERS WHO WILL BE ABLE TO DEMONSTRATE THE NECESSARY PROFESSIONALISM REQUIRED TO COMPETE AND INTERACT EFFECTIVELY WITH MAJOR INDUSTRY PLAYERS. A NEW DYNASTY IS BEING CREATED WHICH WILL NOT JUST EXPLOIT THE REGION'S CREATIVE POTENTIAL IN THE MOST EFFECTIVE WAY, BUT WHICH WILL GENERATE ECONOMIC RETURNS THAT WILL BE PLOUGHED DIRECTLY BACK INTO THE CULTURAL INFRASTRUCTURE.

CONTACT:
Phil Ellis
W http://www.manchester-city-coll.ac.uk/rawfish
E rawfish@manchester-city-coll.ac.uk
T +44(0)161 957 1792
F +44(0)161 957 1742

Example: Jonny produces and presents a successful jazz flavoured night. Marcus and Jamal promote drum 'n' bass night Guidance, voted the Manchester best club night. Darren promotes some of the most successful acts in the UK at the Witchwood near Manchester.

52

RAW FISH records

Raw Fish Records
Paul Cunningham, Phil Bennett
Niall M. Jerveys
The Design Unit, City College Manchester
UK
126 x 126 mm, 5 x 5 in

Designed to promote Raw Fish Records, this work is from one in a series of six packs designed to promote businesses connected with the recording and performance industries. The plastic wallet contains business and record listings, educational information, a CD Rom, a keyring, and business cards.

COOKFREEZE

APTLY NAMED REHEARSAL ROOMS
EMERGING FROM A REDUNDANT KITCHEN.
THIS STATE-OF-THE-ART BUILDING IS NOW
EQUIPPED AND READY FOR PROFESSIONAL
MUSIC SESSIONS. A MULTI-MEDIA
SUITE AND MEETING PLACE PROVIDE AN
ENVIRONMENT READY TO MAKE MUSIC.

THE COOKFREEZE IS AVAILABLE FOR
EXTERNAL HIRE BUT ALSO AS A REGULAR
SPACE FOR THOSE INVOLVED IN THE
COURSES.

Contact: Paul O'Brien or Jim Powell
+44 (0)161 740 9438 or +44 (0)161 740 1491 x 360

The Team

Adrian Armstrong
Creator, technologist, musician and producer.
Provides the strategic vision and implements the educational
and business input for the centre.

Phil Ellis Manager
Co-ordinates Music and New Media Management and manages
the label and the business elements. Twenty years experience
in the industry working with a variety of bands and projects.
Later signed a worldwide deal with Virgin, Chrysalis, BMG, EMI, Arista,
All Around the World, Warner Chappell, Peer Music and
Tuppachic to name a few. Phil has also been responsible for
successful dance records in the UK and Europe.

Martin Moscrop
Member of ACR (A Certain Ratio) signed to the famous Factory
label. Martin has played a major role in the Manchester sound
of the eighties and influenced developing bands in the nineties.
Later signed a worldwide deal with A & M records as well as
producing and remixing many artists. Martin coordinates the
National Diploma and Certificate and runs the A&R division of
Raw Fish.

Richard Hollywood
Manages Performance Technology. Former CBS Studio
Recording and Digital Mastering engineer. Richard has worked
with a wide variety of recording artists, including Roachford,
Opera Singer Placido Domingo, composer Jerry Goldsmith and
Terence Trent Darby. He has also worked in Melbourne as a
Studio Operations Manager for Radio Australia.

Paul O'Brien
Manager of the facilities and studios. Paul's role is proactive,
attending to the commercial aspect of the production output.
He is a producer and sound engineer and has worked with
many artists in the UK and abroad.

Plus many more people, such as Duncan, Paul, Jason, Samantha,
Clare, Mike, Chris, Steve, Andy, Dingo, Tom, Christophe and Mark.

53

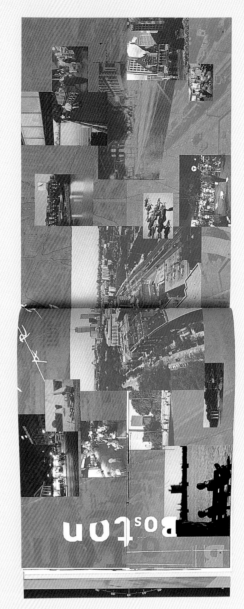

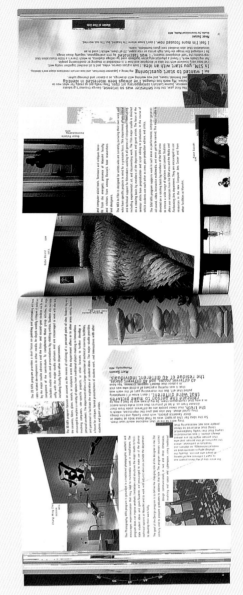

TITLE: **Mass College of Art '97–'99 Catalog**

DESIGNER/S: **Tammy Dotson, Wing Ngan, Angelia Geyer, Clifford Stoltze**

ART DIRECTOR/S: **Clifford Stoltze**

PHOTOGRAPHER/S: **Guy Michel Telemague, Michael Cogliantry, Oscar Palacio, Daniel Szabo**

DESIGN COMPANY: **Stoltze Design**

COUNTRY OF ORIGIN: **USA**

PAGE DIMENSIONS: **279 x 203 mm, 11 x 8 in**

WORK DESCRIPTION: **The '97–'99 MassArt Catalog was intended to reflect the diversity of both the student population and the educational experience at the Massachusetts College of Art. A balance between high-tech and craft styles was achieved by combining computer technology with handmade artwork to create an irregular design in collage form.**

massachusetts
college of
ART

FIG. 33

TITLE: **Promotional Book '98–'99**
DESIGNER/S: **Fabio Berruti**
PHOTOGRAPHER/S: **Fabio Berruti**
DESIGN COMPANY: **Infinite Studio**
COUNTRY OF ORIGIN: **Italy**
PAGE DIMENSIONS: **300 x 200 mm, 11³/₄ x 7³/₄ in**

WORK DESCRIPTION:
**Self-promotional brochure, Christmas greetings,
and calendar. loosely bound together with hand
made, plumbed string.**

photography
fotografia

portrait
live stage
still life
stock archivio

graphic design
design grafico

packaging design
logos
special box
collane tematiche
merchandising design

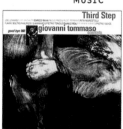

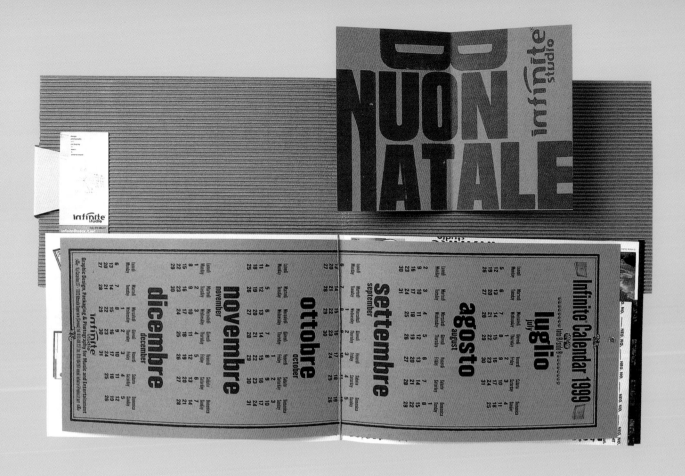

infinite studio®

Il lavoro di Infinite Studio è stato riconosciuto internazionalmente attraverso premi e pubblicazioni di alto prestigio.
All' "European Design Annual" istituito dalla rivista americana Print e dall'editore Roto Vision, Infinite Studio è stato selezionato e premiato nel 1997 e 1998 come studio di design grafico/packaging e Fabio Berruti come designer.
L'editore inglese Duncan Baird e l'autore Roger Walton hanno selezionato alcuni lavori di Infinite Studio da inserire nei volumi "Sight for Sound" - interamente dedicato alla grafica e packaging per la musica - e "Typographics 3: Global Vision" dedicato alle nuove e più interessanti proposte di design grafico dell'attuale panorama mondiale.
Negli Stati Uniti, dove il "Creativity Award" è ormai un'istituzione dal 1971, Infinite Studio è stato premiato con l'Award of Distinction e l'inserimento nel "Creativity Annual 27" per due lavori realizzati nel 1997.
La rivista coreana "Monthly Design" in un numero monografico sul design in Italia ha dedicato un ampio articolo su Infinite Studio dal titolo "Keeping the Heritage of Raffaello".

1. "Monthly Design - Design Venture in Italia" (Agosto 1998) Corea
2. "Print - European Regional Design Annual 1997" (Marzo/Aprile 1997 - edizione europea)
3. "Print - Print's European Design Annual 1998" (Marzo/Aprile 1998 - edizione europea)
4. "Print - European Regional Design Annual 1997" (edizione U.S.A.)
5. "Print - European Design Annual 1998" (edizione U.S.A.)
6. "Sight for Sound" by Roger Walton
Duncan Baird Publishers (Londra 1997)
7. "Anima Fragile" Vasco Rossi (BMG Ricordi 1997) presente nel volume: "Typographics 3: Global Vision" Duncan Baird Publishers (Londra 1998)

SURF HOUSE
International Distribution Internationale
1998 1999

FREESTYLE DIRECTIONAL	150	155	159	
Overall Length	1490	1540	1590	
Running Length	1120	1160	1200	
Nose Width	284.9	288.9	1200	
Waist Width	242	245	292	
Tail Width	284.5	245	247	
Nose Length	200	288.5	291.7	
Tail Length	170	205	210	
Nose Height	47	175	180	
Tail Height	43	50	53	
MAX Stance Width	575	45	48	
MIN Stance Width	415	590	615	
Stance Set Back	20	430	455	
		25	30	All spec measurements are in millimeters (mm.)

THE PRINCE OF RIDE

BASE DESIGN

To enhance its all-round performance
the FSD series comes with a blazingly
fast P-tex Electra 2000 base

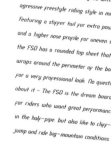

The newest shape in the always-progressive
T&C line, the FSD was designed with an
aggressive freestyle riding style in mind.
Featuring a stiffer tail for extra power
and a higher nose profile for uneven snow,
the FSD has a rounded top sheet that
wraps around the perimeter of the board
for a very professional look. No question
about it - The FSD is the dream board
for riders who want great performance
in the half-pipe, but also like to cliff-
jump and ride big-mountain conditions.

CONSTRUCTION

Featuring a full length wood core that stretches from
tip to tail and from edge to edge, the FSD offers an
incredibly lively ride whether in the halfpipe, the
terrain park or in the powder. The FSD also boasts
full wraparound edges at tip and tail, an extra
layer of fibreglass under the edges and
stainless steel inserts with a 4X4 pattern.

FREESTYLE DIRECTI

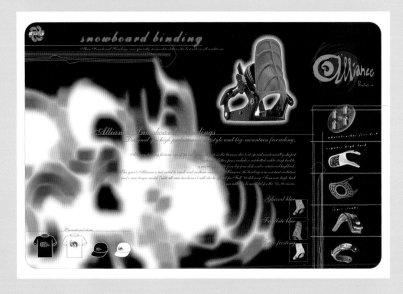

TITLE:	SurfPolitix Trade Show Brochure	WORK DESCRIPTION:	Brochure for Surfpolitix,
DESIGNER/S:	Marc Serre, Michel Valois,		a manufacturer of snowboards.
	George Fok, Bob Beck		The brochure reflects the company's
ART DIRECTOR/S:	Marc Serre, Daniel Fortin,		wish to counter the present trend for
	George Fok		garish colors and aggressive, cyber-
ILLUSTRATOR/S:	Marc Serre, George Fok		style graphics with a more refined,
PHOTOGRAPHER/S:	Scalp, Philippe Roger		contemporary look for its products.
DESIGN COMPANY:	Époxy		
COUNTRY OF ORIGIN:	Canada		
PAGE DIMENSIONS:	432 x 279 mm, 17 x 11 in		

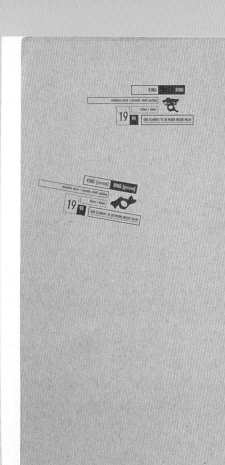

RING ___ RING
stainless steel / ceramic shell casting
19 | 94 | 50mm x 60mm | ONE ELEMENT TO BE WORN INSIDE PALM

RING [EDITION] ___ RING [EDITION]
stainless steel / ceramic shell casting
19 | 95 | 62mm x 80mm | ONE ELEMENT TO BE WORN INSIDE PALM

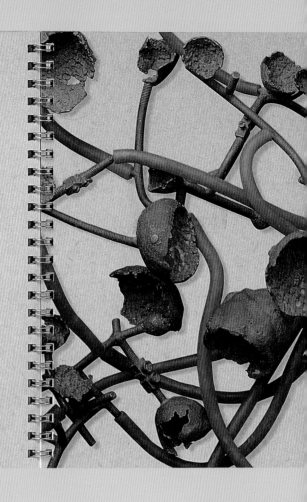

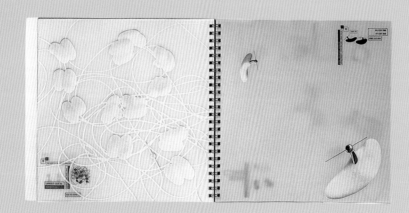

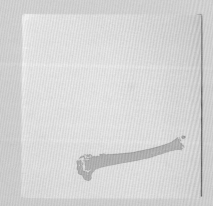

TITLE: Christoph Zellweger
DESIGNER/S: Dom Raban, Pat Walker
PHOTOGRAPHER/S: Christoph Zellweger
DESIGN COMPANY: Eg.G
COUNTRY OF ORIGIN: UK
PAGE DIMENSIONS: 210 x 210 mm, 8³/₈ x 8³/₈ in
WORK DESCRIPTION: Catalog for jeweler Christoph
Zellweger, featuring a variety
of papers and printing techniques
specially selected to reflect and
complement his work.

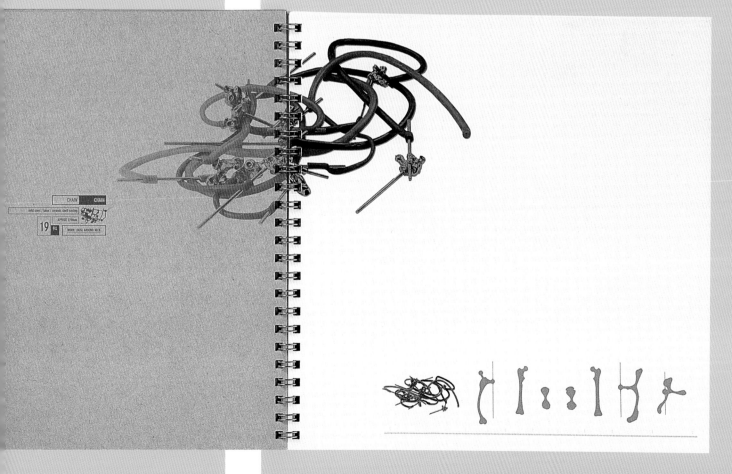

61

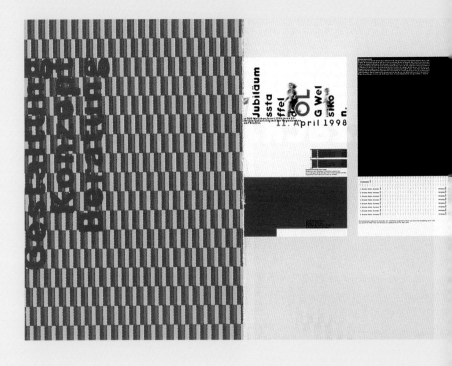

TITLE   Grafiktraktor
DESIGNER   Thomas Bruggisser
DESIGN COMPANY   Grafiktraktor
COUNTRY OF ORIGIN   Switzerland
PAGE DIMENSIONS   60 x 80 mm, 2^3/$_8$ x 3^3/$_8$ in
WORK DESCRIPTION   Self- promotional brochure

Thomas Bruggisser
Grafiktraktor ¡
Metzggasse 8
8400 Winterthur
T 052 212 31 00
F 052 212 31 02

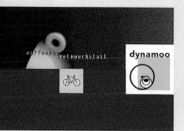

Here, and previous spread

Mohawk Paper Mills: Your Name Here
Paula Scher, Anke Stohlmann,
Keith Daigle
Paula Scher
Pentagram Design
USA
280 x 288 mm, 11 x 11⅓ in

Unlike the usual material designed
to promote paper, this swatchbook
pokes fun at the way in which
designers take themselves too
seriously. This work gives people
the chance to cannibalize its
contents without guilt or shame –
it is a "cheat sheet" for designers.

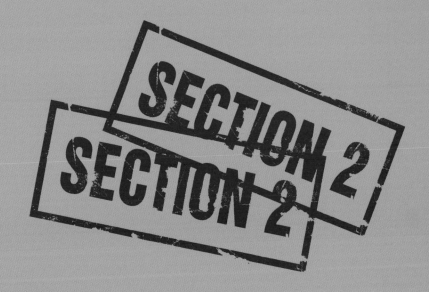

SECTION 2
SECTION 2

CULTURAL

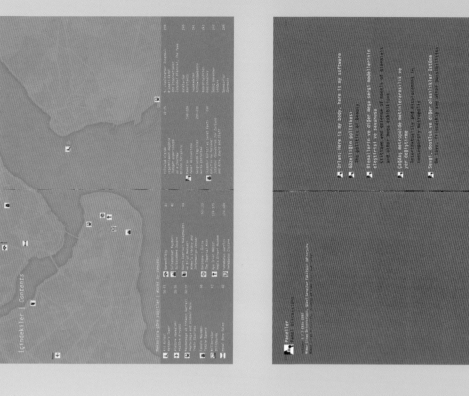

yaşam, güzellik,
on life, beauty,
çeviriler/aktarımlar ve
translations and
diğer güçlükler üstüne
other difficulties

TITLE: 5th International Istanbul
Biennial Book

DESIGNER/S: Gülizar Çepoğlu, Aysun Pelvan

ART DIRECTOR/S: Gülizar Çepoğlu

PHOTOGRAPHER/S: Murat Germen, Ekmel Ertan,
Cem Akkan

DESIGN COMPANY: Gülizar Çepoğlu Design Co.

COUNTRY OF ORIGIN: Turkey

PAGE DIMENSIONS: 165 x 230 mm, 6½ x 9⅛ in

WORK DESCRIPTION:

Second of two books documenting the 5th International
Istanbul Biennial. Printed after the event, its aim was
to reflect the spirit of the exhibition and the host city as
expressed in the subtitle: *On Life, Beauty, Translations
and Other Difficulties.*

Lotty Rosenfeld
İstanbul'daki sanat gösterisi
(5 Ekim 1997) ve video
gösteriminden.
From the actions performed in
İstanbul (October 5th. 1997)
and video screening.

71

"(...) 'She in the Outer Space' is a simulation of a module of a spaceship. It contains both the bedroom and the bathroom of a female astronaut. Everything is very simple and elementary. The vital necessities of a person of the female sex is reduced to her personal hygiene and her place of rest. (...) I use the exterior space like a metaphor : A space without time and gravity. A place which collects the fluctuations of thoughts, where the abstract ideas co-exist with the physical necessities, a place where the stars are travel companions and illuminate the unknown."

Ana Laura Aláez

"(...) 'Uzaydaki Kız' bir uzay kapsülü simülasyonudur. İçinde bir astronot kızın hem yatak odası, hem de banyosu bulunmaktadır. Her şey çok basittir ve temel ihtiyaçlara göre düzenlenmiştir. Bir kadının tüm yaşamsal gereksinimleri, onun kişisel hijyeni ve dinlenme alanıyla sınırlanmıştır. (...) Burada uzayı bir metafor olarak kullanıyorum: Zamansız ve yerçekimsiz bir mekan. Düşüncenin titreşimlerini toplayan, soyut düşüncelerin fiziksel gereksinimlerle yanyana varolduğu bir yer. Burada yıldızlar yol arkadaşlığı yaparlar ve bilinmeyeni aydınlatırlar."

Ana Laura Aláez

Ana Laura Aláez
"Uzaydaki Kız", 1997.
"She in the Outer Space".
Yerleştirme.
Installation.

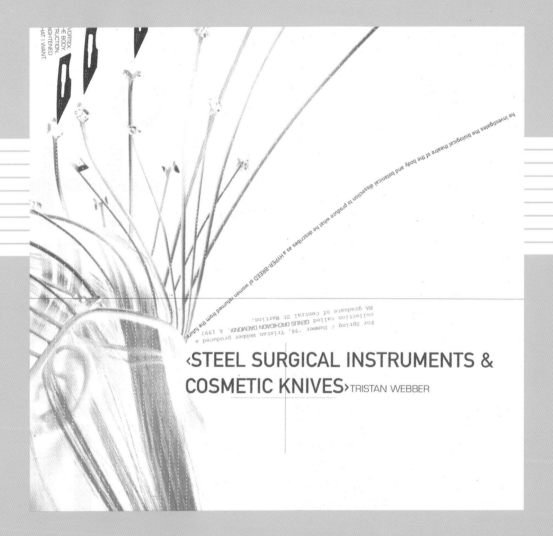

‹STEEL SURGICAL INSTRUMENTS &
COSMETIC KNIVES›TRISTAN WEBBER

For Spring / Summer '98, Tristan Webber produced a
collection called GENUS ORCHIDAON DAEMONIX. A 1997
MA graduate of Central St Martins,
he investigates the biological theatre of the body and botanical dissection to produce what he describes as a HYPER-BREED of women returned from the future.

TITLE	**Enhance 57:19**	**198 x 210 mm, 7³/₄ x 8¹/₄ in**
DESIGNERS	**Peter Maybury**	**Fold-out fashion magazine consisting**
ART DIRECTORS	**Peter Maybury, Ian Sen**	**of two 594 x 420 mm (23³/₈ x 16¹/₂ in)**
PHOTOGRAPHERS	**Gavin Fernandez, Chris Moore**	**sheets that fold into 12 pages. This**
DESIGN COMPANY	**Peter Maybury**	**edition of 500 copies was sent out**
COUNTRY OF ORIGIN	**Ireland/England**	**in clear plastic covers.**

<Enhance 57:19>

57 / 500

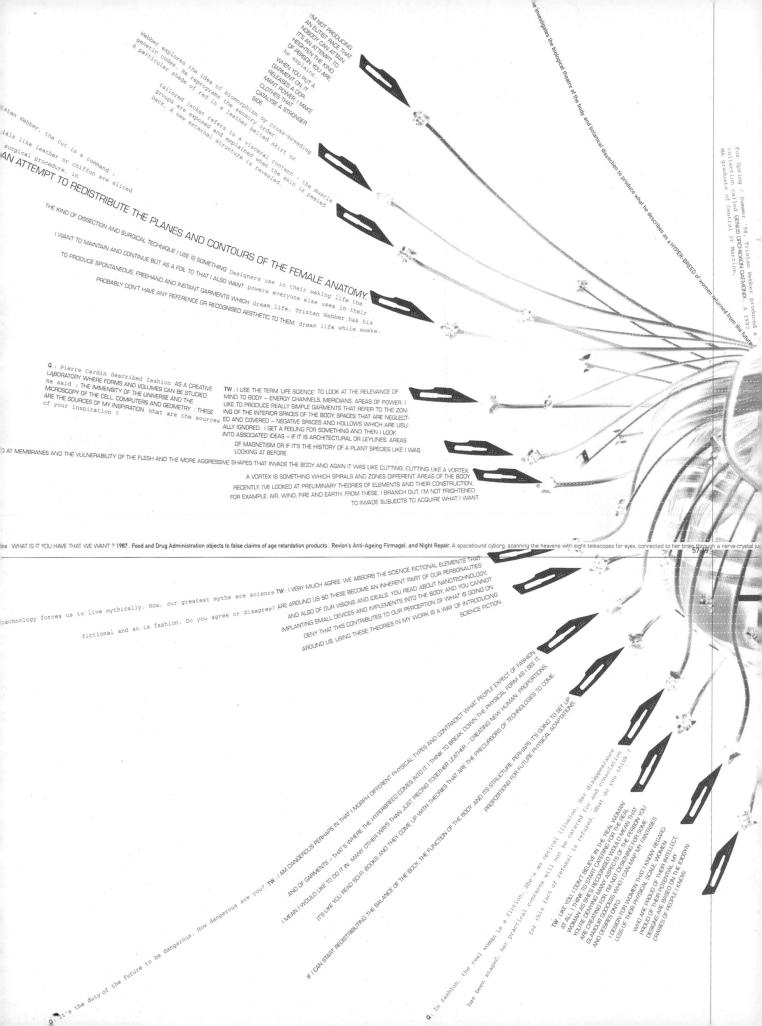

I'M NOT PRODUCING AN ELITIST RACE THAT NOBODY CAN ATTAIN. IT'S AN ATTEMPT TO HEIGHTEN THE KIND OF PERSON YOU ARE, he explains. WHEN YOU PUT A GARMENT ON, IT RELEASES A DOR-MANT POWER. I MAKE CLOTHES THAT CATALYSE A STRONGER SIDE.

Webber explores the idea of biomorphism. He reprograms the genetic codes. A particular shade of red in a leather belted skirt or tailored jacket refers to a visceral content - the muscle groups are exposed and explained when the skin is peeled back. A new external structure is revealed.

...stan Webber, the cut is a command :
...ials like leather or chiffon are sliced
...surgical procedure, in

AN ATTEMPT TO REDISTRIBUTE THE PLANES AND CONTOURS OF THE FEMALE ANATOMY.

THE KIND OF DISSECTION AND SURGICAL TECHNIQUE I USE IS SOMETHING Designers use in their waking life the
I WANT TO MAINTAIN AND CONTINUE BUT AS A FOIL TO THAT I ALSO WANT powers everyone else uses in their
TO PRODUCE SPONTANEOUS, FREEHAND AND INSTANT GARMENTS WHICH dream life. Tristan Webber has his
PROBABLY DON'T HAVE ANY REFERENCE OR RECOGNISED AESTHETIC TO THEM. dream life while awake.

...investigates the biological theatre of the body and botanical dissection to produce what he describes as a HYPER-BREED of women returned from the future.

For Spring / Summer '98, Tristan Webber produced a collection called GENUS ORCHIDION DAEMONIX. A 1997 MA graduate of Central St Martins,

Q : Pierre Cardin described fashion AS A CREATIVE LABORATORY WHERE FORMS AND VOLUMES CAN BE STUDIED. He said : THE IMMENSITY OF THE UNIVERSE AND THE MICROSCOPY OF THE CELL, COMPUTERS AND GEOMETRY : THESE ARE THE SOURCES OF MY INSPIRATION. What are the sources of your inspiration ?

TW : I USE THE TERM 'LIFE SCIENCE' TO LOOK AT THE RELEVANCE OF MIND TO BODY – ENERGY CHANNELS, MERIDIANS, AREAS OF POWER. I LIKE TO PRODUCE REALLY SIMPLE GARMENTS THAT REFER TO THE ZON-ING OF THE INTERIOR SPACES OF THE BODY, SPACES THAT ARE NEGLECT-ED AND COVERED – NEGATIVE SPACES AND HOLLOWS WHICH ARE USU-ALLY IGNORED. I GET A FEELING FOR SOMETHING AND THEN I LOOK INTO ASSOCIATED IDEAS – IF IT IS ARCHITECTURAL OR LEYLINES, AREAS OF MAGNETISM OR IF IT'S THE HISTORY OF A PLANT SPECIES LIKE I WAS LOOKING AT BEFORE.

...D AT MEMBRANES AND THE VULNERABILITY OF THE FLESH AND THE MORE AGGRESSIVE SHAPES THAT INVADE THE BODY AND AGAIN IT WAS LIKE CUTTING, CUTTING LIKE A VORTEX. A VORTEX IS SOMETHING WHICH SPIRALS AND ZONES DIFFERENT AREAS OF THE BODY. RECENTLY, I'VE LOOKED AT PRELIMINARY THEORIES OF ELEMENTS AND THEIR CONSTRUCTION, FOR EXAMPLE, AIR, WIND, FIRE AND EARTH. FROM THESE, I BRANCH OUT. I'M NOT FRIGHTENED TO INVADE SUBJECTS TO ACQUIRE WHAT I WANT.

...ks : WHAT IS IT YOU HAVE THAT WE WANT ? 1987 : Food and Drug Administration objects to false claims of age retardation products : Revlon's Anti-Ageing Firmagel, and Night Repair. A spacebound cyborg, scanning the heavens with eight telescopes for eyes, connected to her brain through a nerve-crystal ju

technology forces us to live mythically. Now, our greatest myths are science TW : I VERY MUCH AGREE. WE ABSORB THE SCIENCE FICTIONAL ELEMENTS THAT
fictional and so is fashion. Do you agree or disagree? ARE AROUND US SO THESE BECOME AN INHERENT PART OF OUR PERSONALITIES AND ALSO OF OUR VISIONS AND IDEALS. YOU READ ABOUT NANOTECHNOLOGY, IMPLANTING SMALL DEVICES AND IMPLEMENTS INTO THE BODY, AND YOU CANNOT DENY THAT THIS CONTRIBUTES TO OUR PERCEPTION OF WHAT IS GOING ON AROUND US. USING THESE THEORIES IN MY WORK IS A WAY OF INTRODUCING SCIENCE FICTION.

TW : I AM DANGEROUS PERHAPS IN THAT I MORPH DIFFERENT PHYSICAL TYPES AND CONTRADICT WHAT PEOPLE EXPECT OF FASHION
AND OF GARMENTS – THAT'S WHERE THE HYPERBREED COMES INTO IT. I THINK TO BREAK DOWN THE PHYSICAL FORM AS I SEE IT,
I MEAN I WOULD LIKE TO DO IT IN MANY OTHER WAYS THAN JUST PIECING TOGETHER LEATHER – CREATING NEW HUMAN PROPORTIONS.
IT'S LIKE YOU READ SCI-FI BOOKS AND THEY COME UP WITH THEORIES THAT ARE THE PRECURSORS OF TECHNOLOGIES TO COME.
IT'S LIKE REDISTRIBUTING THE BALANCE OF THE BODY, THE FUNCTION OF THE BODY AND ITS STRUCTURE. PERHAPS IT'S GOING TO SET UP PROPOSITIONS FOR FUTURE PHYSICAL ADAPTATIONS.

TW : LIKE YOU, I DON'T BELIEVE IN THE REAL WOMAN AT ALL. I THINK TO START CATERING FOR THE REAL WOMAN AS SHE'S RECOGNISED WOULD MEAN THAT YOU'RE DENYING MANY ASPECTS OF THE PERSON YOU ARE CREATING FOR. I'M NOT DESIGNING FOR SOME GLAMOUR GODDESS WHO I CAN MAP MY FANTASIES AND DESIRES ONTO. I DESIGN FOR WOMEN THAT I KNOW REGARD. WHO ARE PROUD OF THEIR INTELLECT. LESS OF THEIR PHYSICAL SCALE. WOMEN PROUD OF THEIR POTENTIAL. MY DESIGNS ARE BASED ON THE IDIOSYN-CRASIES OF PEOPLE I KNOW.

...it's the duty of the future to be dangerous. How dangerous are you?

Q : In fashion, the real woman is a fiction. She's an optical illusion. Her disappearance has been staged. her practical concerns will not be catered for and consolation for this fact of refusal is refused. What do you think ?

the base of her skull. 1988 : A sixty-three percent rise is plastic surgery is reported. The magic is weakening and many of the dreamers are stirring discontentedly. 1989 : Cindy Crawford signs a \$4 million, four year deal with Revlon. I'm having illusions.

œ ‡ °

Q:Fashion is metamorphosis into
compressed image. It's
a refusal of narcissism, the
tragedy of being totally… me.
How do you define fashion ?

TW: FASHION IS COMPLETELY IMPOSSIBLE TO DEFINE BECAUSE IT'S SO TRANSIENT. IT'S OFTEN MASTURBATORY.
FASHION IS SO ALLURING AT THE MOMENT. I FIND IT VERY FRUSTRATING. THE VISION THAT I HAVE WHEN I START.
FULFILLING THAT AND THE BARRIERS I COME ACROSS TECHNICAL AND FINANCIAL BARRIERS. SOMETIMES IT'S
DIFFICULT TO GAIN THE INFORMATION YOU NEED TO MAKE CLOTHES. FASHION IS A SERVICE INDUSTRY.

Q: Pierre Cardin described couture as A CREATIVE LABORATORY WHERE FORMS AND VOLUMES CAN BE STUDIED. He said 'THE IMMENSITY OF THE UNIVERSE AND THE MICROSCOPY OF THE CELL, COMPUTERS AND GEOMETRY THESE ARE THE SOURCES OF MY INSPIRATION'. What are the main sources of your inspiration ?

OG: IT CHANGES, IT CHANGES ALL THE TIME. AT FIRST I DID A RETROSPECTIVE BUT THINGS GET RECYCLED AND RECYCLED AND IT JUST GETS DULL. THE INSECTS COLLECTION WAS REALLY IMPERSONAL AND I COULD THINK ABOUT WHAT I WANTED OUT OF INSECTS TO MAKE CLOTHES. I DID A DOGS-TOOTH PRINT THAT LOOKED LIKE BEETLES. IT WAS ONE OF THE NICEST THINGS I DID.

Q: Insects are interesting. Most people thought that robots of the future would look like C3PO but they actually look more like cockroaches. For Spring / Summer 1997, your CLOCKWORK DRAGONZ collection contained an A-LINE ROBOT DRESS. What did this look like ?

OG: IT WAS A DRESS WITH VENTS MATCHED WITH A JACKET TURNED BACK TO FRONT. WE DID TROUSERS IN ROBOT SHAPES – FITTED ALONG THE THIGH AND THEN JUTTING OUT AT THE BACK OF THE KNEE. TO HAVE SOMETHING JUTTING OUT OF THE BODY LIKE THAT WAS AMAZING AND IT WAS ELEGANT. THE ROBOTS COLLECTION WAS SIMILAR TO THE INSECTS ONE. I PICKED AN INANIMATE OBJECT WITH A HISTORY BEHIND IT.

Q: I like your choice of the image of the robot. In the 50s, Marshall McLuhan wrote an book called THE MECHANICAL BRIDE after he noticed images of robotic, automated women in adverts - like the ads for nylon tights with lines of kicking legs moving up and down on an automated machine.

OG: IMAGES
OF
AUTOMATED
WOMEN
ARE
EVERYWHERE
NOW.

Q: For Autumn / Winter 1997, you did a collection called CHOPPER. What was that about ?

OG: CHOPPER IS A METAPHOR FOR THE FUSION OF TRADITION AND INVENTION IN COUTURE TECHNIQUES AND IN STYLE – THE SALON MIXED WITH THE STREET, HISTORY MIXED WITH THE FUTURE. CHOPPER WAS REALLY HARD WORK BOTH TECHNICALLY AND CONCEPTUALLY. THAT COLLECTION WAS ONE OF THE MOST UNPLEASANT THINGS I HAD TO DO BUT IT WAS ONE OF THE BEST SHOWS I'VE DONE AND IT SOLD REALLY WELL BECAUSE IT WAS WEARABLE.

Q: On the surface of it, wearability wouldn't seem to be a priority with you. Is wearability important to you ?

OG: IT'S VERY IMPORTANT. THAT'S WHERE THE GENIUS IS, THAT'S WHAT IT'S ABOUT. I HOPE TO CHANGE OPINIONS OF WHAT IS WEARABLE. THERE IS DEFINITELY SOMETHING MISSING OUT THERE. PEOPLE ARE AFTER SOMETHING THAT IS ORIGINAL, WORKED ON AND BEAUTIFUL.

Q: Hussein Chalayan says that EVERYTHING IS WEARABLE. Would you agree or disagree ?

OG: NO. WEARABLE TO WHO ? FASHION ISN'T ABOUT ART. IT'S ABOUT PUSHING THINGS FORWARD AND MORE THAN EVER IT'S ABOUT PEOPLE WEARING IT AND DOING WHAT THEY WANT.

Q: Is it true that you were the first designer to use Jungle soundtracking in your catwalk shows ?

OG: I THINK SO. ALL THE JUNGLE SOUNDTRACKS I USE ARE WRITTEN SPECIFICALLY FOR THE SHOWS BY THIS GUY CALLED BLUZ IN BRIGHTON. HE'S GOT A RECORD DEAL NOW AND THE SHOW SOUNDTRACKS WILL BE RELEASED. BLUZ HAS DONE MY SOUNDTRACKS SINCE THE TITANIC SHOW.

Q: How do you collaborate on the soundtracks ?

OG: I TELL HIM WHAT THE COLLECTION IS ABOUT AND HE GOES AWAY AND COMPOSES THE MUSIC. THE TITANIC ONE WAS SO GOOD. HE USED HORNS ON IT. IT WAS REALLY SIMILAR TO WHAT DOC SCOTT DOES BUT IT HAD MORE OF A STORY TO IT. THE LAST ONE DIDN'T WORK OUT AS WELL. I WANTED A TRACK THAT FELT EXACTLY LIKE BEING ON VALIUM OR TEMAZEPAM.

Q: What's the forthcoming soundtrack going to be like ?

OG: IT'S LIKE AN IRRITATING BENNY HILL GANGSTER TUNE. IT'S LIKE REALLY DARK JUMP-UP CHOPPED APART. WE'LL BE USING RAGGA GOLD JEWELLERY. I SUPPOSE IT'S A PLAYFUL THEFT OF CULTURE REALLY.

Q: What music are you listening to at the moment ?

OG: JUNGLE. I LISTEN TO IT ON THE RADIO OR WHATEVER COMES ALONG. JUNGLE IS REALLY IMPORTANT. THE WAY IT'S CONSTRUCTED AND THE WAY IT WORKS. THERE ISN'T ANY ONE JUNGLE. IN THREE MONTHS TIME, SOMEONE WILL COME ALONG AND DO SOMETHING COMPLETELY NEW. I LIKE THE TURNOVER IN JUNGLE AND PEOPLE CAN SURVIVE IN IT.

Q: Technology is embedded in the fabrics you choose for your designs. Can you tell me more about your fabrics ?

OG: I USE 50% MODERN FABRICS AND 50% TRADITIONAL. I ONCE USED A WAFFLE LYCRA IN SHINY BLACK AND WHITE AND IN THE LAST COLLECTION I USED THERMOCHROMIC PVC WHICH DOESN'T SELL. THERE WAS A LOT OF INTEREST IN IT BUT PEOPLE JUST WON'T WEAR IT. I ALSO USED THIS GREAT LYCRA I FOUND IN THAILAND.

onto the dry areas of just dried skin. 1981 : Ultima II emerges with a stable water-soluble collagen skin cream. The cosmetics consultant wore a white lab coat. Her English was excellent, and her manner had that ingrained remoteness and casual as

Q: In TITANIC, you emphasised the backbone rather than the shoulder as in previous collections. What did these garments look like ?

OG: WE DID WOOL JUMPERS WITH KNITTED SPINES AND JACKETS THAT CREASE INWARDS AT THE BACK.

A frolicking of joints, the musical angle which the arm makes with the forearm, a foot that fails, a knee that bends, fingers that seem to fly off the hand - all of this is like a perpetual play of images in which the parts of the human body seem to send each other gestures, musical phrases, in which the notes of the DJ's vinyl (the atmosphere of the runway soundtrack) evoke the idea of a giant insector. The females themselves provide the beating wings.

Images of automated women are ev

METAMORPHOSIS autumn / winter 1995 / 96

TITANIC spring / summer 1996

ZOOMING autumn / winter 1996

CLOCKWORK DRAGONZ spring / summer 1997

CHOP autumn / winter 1997 / 1998

Owen Gaster graduated from Epsom College of Art & Design in 1992. He presented his debut runway collection in February 1994. He currently lives on a farm and continues to produce visions of the future in the form of garments.

OWEN GASTER
<A DIAMOND
EYED TIME CHILD
THIRTY CENTURIES
OLD>

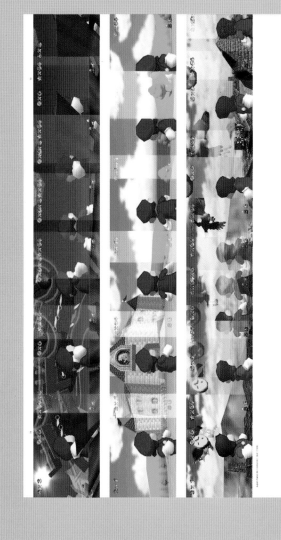

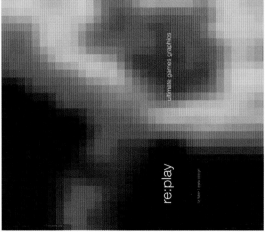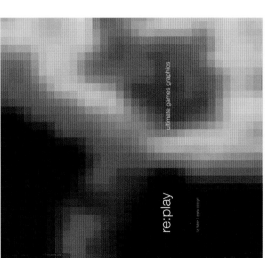

TITLE:	**Re:play – Ultimate Game Graphics**
DESIGNER/S:	**Mark Breslin, Mark Hough,**
	Philip O'Dwyer
PHOTOGRAPHER/S:	**Mark Breslin, Mark Hough,**
	Philip O'Dwyer
DESIGN COMPANY:	**State**
COUNTRY OF ORIGIN:	**UK**
PAGE DIMENSIONS:	**240 x 270 mm, 9¹/₂ x 10⁵/₈ in**
WORK DESCRIPTION:	**Book documenting the development**
	of computer games and their
	increasingly sophisticated graphics.

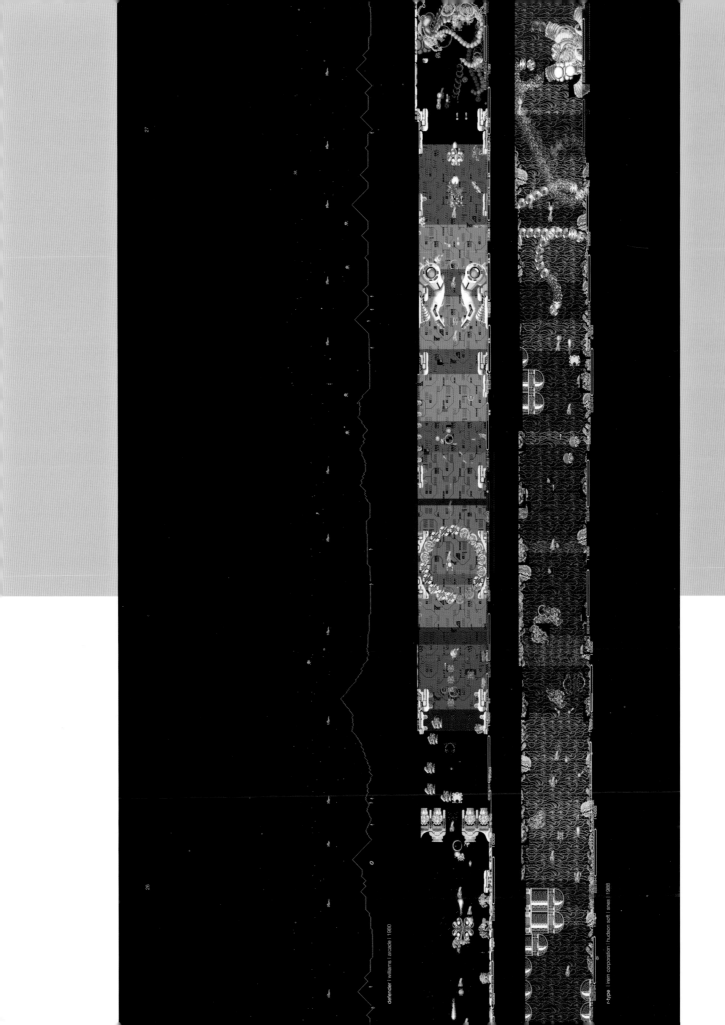

defender | williams | arcade | 1980

r-type | irem corporation | hudson soft | snes | 1988

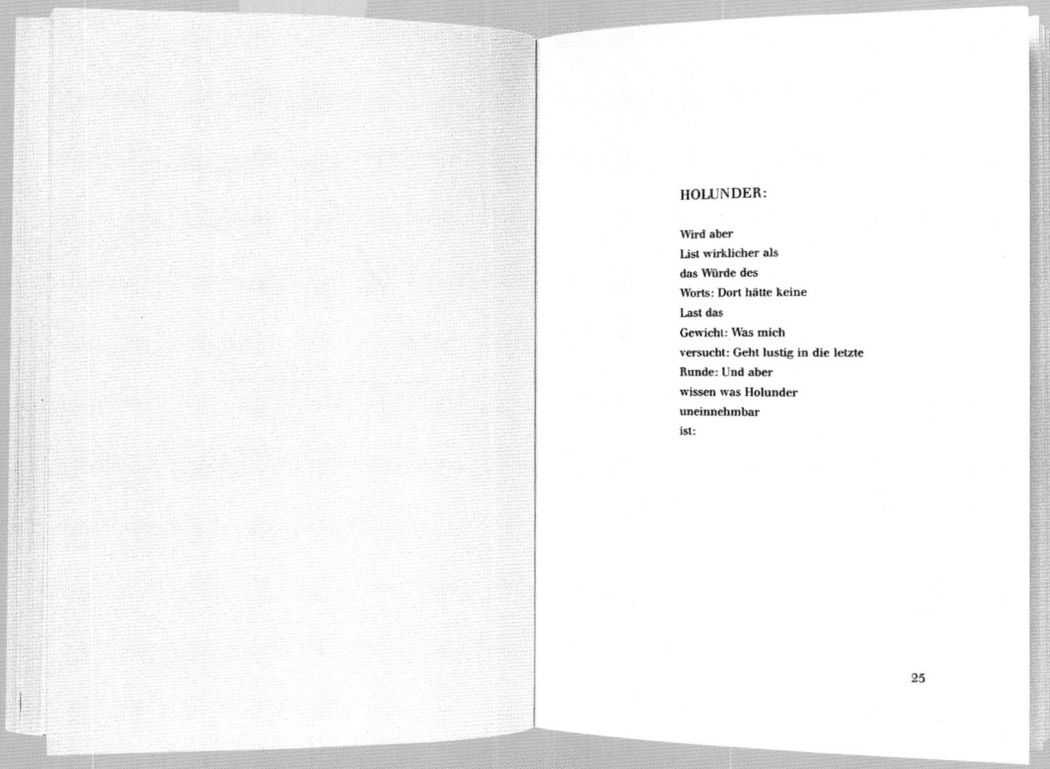

HOLUNDER:

Wind aber
List wirklicher als
das Würde des
Worts: Dort hätte keine
Last das
Gewicht: Was mich
versucht: Geht lustig in die letzte
Runde: Und aber
wissen was Holunder
uneinnehmbar
ist:

25

INGOLD/LEHMANN

TITLE: **Zeichensatz**
DESIGNER/S: **Ann Holyoke Lehmann**
DESIGN COMPANY: **Ann Holyoke Lehmann**
COUNTRY OF ORIGIN: **Germany**
PAGE DIMENSIONS: **170 x 240 mm, 6⅝ x 9½ in**
WORK DESCRIPTION: **Book of twelve silkscreen prints by the designer, each accompanying a poem by Felix Philipp Ingold. The prints were inspired by Ann's own wooden wall sculpture *Signs* (1992).**

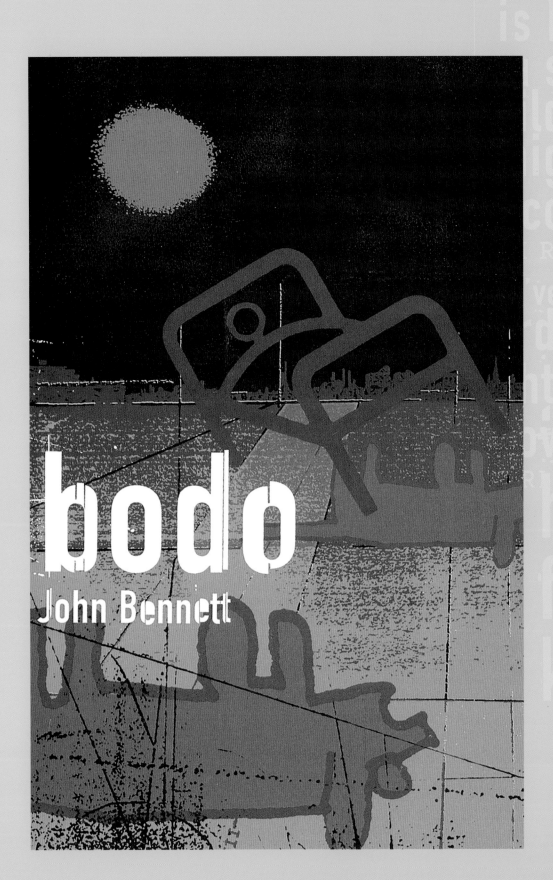

bodo

John Bennett

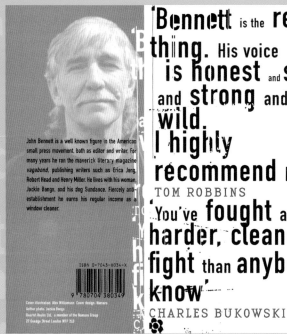

'Bennett is the **real thing.** His voice is **honest** and **smart** and **strong** and a little **wild.** I **highly** recommend him'
TOM ROBBINS

'You've **fought** a **harder, cleaner fight** than **anybody I know**'
CHARLES BUKOWSKI

John Bennett is a well known figure in the American small press movement, both as editor and writer. For many years he ran the maverick literary magazine *vagabond*, publishing writers such as Erica Jong, Robert Head and Henry Miller. He lives with his woman, Jackie Bangs, and his dog Sundance. Fiercely anti-establishment he earns his regular income as a window cleaner.

ISBN 0-7043-8034-X

9 780704 380349

Cover illustration: Alex Williamson. Cover design: Namara
Author photo: Jackie Bangs
Quartet Books Ltd., a member of the Namara Group
27 Goodge Street London W1P 2LD

bodo
John Bennett

bodo
John Bennett

America's most dynamic writer since Kerouac tells the story of one man's rise and fall with a cool eye that misses nothing and never flinches. The hero, Bodo, a German war orphan brought to America by ineffectual foster parents, seems out of place even in his own life. He grows up to become a revered disc jockey, but falls through the cracks of mainstream America and catches up too late with the renegade lifestyles of the sixties.

Scarred in body and psyche by the ravages of World War II, he lives in a state of innocence that is ultimately his undoing.

£9.00

TITLE:	Bodo
DESIGNER/S:	Debbie Holmes
ILLUSTRATOR/S:	Alex Williamson
DESIGN COMPANY:	Namara Design
COUNTRY OF ORIGIN:	UK
PAGE DIMENSIONS:	135 x 210 mm, 5³/₈ x 8³/₈ in
WORK DESCRIPTION:	Cover for the novel
	Bodo by John Bennett.

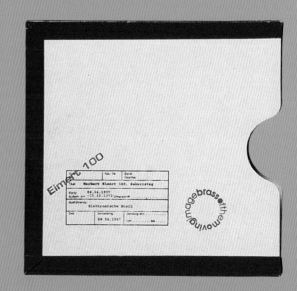

Eimert 100

Aufn.-Nr.		Kat.- Nr.	Band- Geschw.
Titel:	**Herbert Eimert 100. Geburtstag**		
Kontr.	08.04.1897		
Aufgen. am	-15.12.1972 Unterschrift		
Ausführende:	**Elektronische Musik**		
Zeit	Sendefertig 08.04.1997	Sendung am : . . . . von . . . . bis	

imagebrassofthemovingimage

imagebrassofthemovingimage

TITLE:	**Eimert 100**		WORK DESCRIPTION:	**Commemorative book incorporating**
DESIGNER/S:	**Markus Aust, Jörg Oswald**			**the program for a concert performance**
PHOTOGRAPHER/S:	**Dorothea Eimert**			**of contemporary classical music to**
DESIGN COMPANY:	**Televisor**			**mark the 100th anniversary of the birth**
COUNTRY OF ORIGIN:	**Germany**			**of Herbert Eimert. It is presented in an**
PAGE DIMENSIONS:	**170 x 170 mm, 6³/₄ x 6³/₄ in**			**"old-fashioned" reel-to-reel slipcase.**

Eimert/Stockhausen
1952

**Herbert Eimert
Brief an
Karlheinz
Stockhausen
in Paris**

Köln, d. 08.12.52
Lieber Herr Stockhausen,
(...) Ausserdem ist das prinzipielle Interesse des Rundfunks für elektronische Musik gleich null, und es ist schon ein einmaliger Glücksfall, daß wir hier dank der Großzügigkeit des Intendanten, überhaupt auf diesem Gebiet arbeiten können. Vor allem wird es darauf ankommen, die maßgebenden Rundfunkleute davon zu überzeugen, daß solche Arbeiten unbedingt notwendig sind. Was mich immer wieder verwundert und mir eigentlich unbegreiflich ist: daß Sie

dort überhaupt keine elektronischen Klänge kennen und mit Aufnehmen arbeiten, die einem gewissen musikalischen Totalitätsprinzip unterworfen werden, wobei die Grenze der Spielbarkeit in den Bereich der Bandmanipulationen vorverlegt wird und vieles rhythmisch Unspielbare nun mechanisch abläuft. Das kann man mit allen denkbaren Klängen organisieren, es ist ein reines Anwendungsprinzip; man kann es z. B. mit Geigenklängen durchführen, obwohl die Geige ihr eigentliches materiales Wesen ja in der Epoche von Corelli bis Brahms entfaltet hat; man kann es auch mit elektronischen Klängen durchführen, obwohl die elektronischen Klänge sich ihrem Wesen nach in ganz anderer Richtung entfalten werden. Mit solchen Überlegungen möchte ich Sie anregen, auch noch nach andern Gestaltungsprinzipien Ausschau zu halten. Ich habe mir jetzt noch zwei-

mal Ihr Spiel für Orchester angehört (es kommt in der Sendung am 11. Dez. um 23.00 Uhr - Ihre Frau ist darüber unterrichtet!): bei solcher hochorganisierten "Punktmusik" sind die Ein- und Ausschwingvorgänge der Instrumente sehr wesentlich - nimmt man sie weg, und das geschieht ja notwendig bei den barbarischen Bandschnitten, so rollt etwas Mechanisches ab, wie in den rhythmischen Bandstudien von Messiaen und Boulez (die übrigens immer noch nicht angekommen sind). Musikalisch kommen mir diese Versuche wie eine rhythmisierte und dynamisierte Folge von blinden Klängen vor; es ist keine Spur von der ungeheuren Bildhaftigkeit elektronischer Musik darin. Es sind nur auf die Fläche projizierte Strukturen, aber keine klangräumlichen Kristallbildungen, wie sie mir vorschweben. Bei elektronischer Musik ändert sich nämlich der Prozeß des

26

Eimert/Stockhausen
1952

Hörens, das nach "draussen" verlegt wird und auf wirkliche Klangbilder gerichtet ist. Dies verhält sich zur bisherigen Musik wie das Theater zum Film; der Ton wird nicht mehr in dem uns umgebenden Raum gehört. zum erstenmal wird er selbst Raumelement und tritt in dieselbe Distanz zu uns wie der in der Photographie bewegte Gegenstand im Film....

Mit guten Wünschen und besten Grüssen
Ihr Herbert Eimert

27

87

MOUTH FULL

Teeth Flash. A laugh. Cutlery rattles on china. Two lattés and a chardonnay. A cosy couple at table 2. A cool couple in the corner. Know the face. Can't place it. Great hair. A chair scrape, a glass chink, muffled conversation, and one loudmouth near the front. Fingers click. I hate that. Yes sir? Kitchen bell. Ding. Ding. Table nine. Booking? What booking? Oh yeah, table for six. Drinks to start? A fork drops. Camparis' clash. The goat's cheese special smells. Really smells. The wine list sir. I didn't order this. More bread? The number 96 tram clatters past. Wish I was on it.

ST. KILDA IN YOUR FACE

TITLE: St. Kilda in Your Face

DESIGNER/S: Andrew Hoyne

ILLUSTRATOR/S: Alex Tyers

PHOTOGRAPHER/S: Jason Loucas

DESIGN COMPANY: Hoyne Design

COUNTRY OF ORIGIN: Australia

PAGE DIMENSIONS: 258 x 312 mm, 10¹/₈ x 12¹/₄ in

WORK DESCRIPTION: The photographic images, iconic drawings, text, and quotes from this book aim to capture the streetwise essence of the rich diversity of people who live in the innercity district of St. Kilda in Melbourne, Australia.

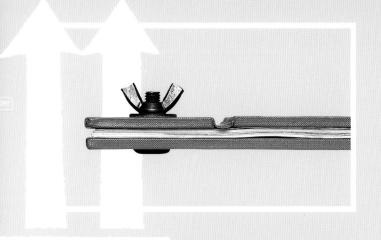

when reality bleeds on off the mind **X** is what remains maybe **X** is pure thought **X** is where thoughts speed up & become more complex to the point where they can leave you behind **X** is where logic becomes emotion.

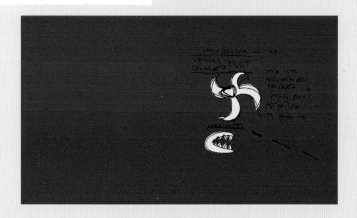

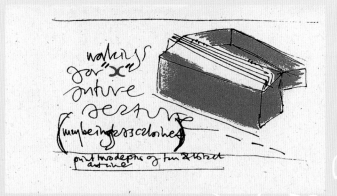

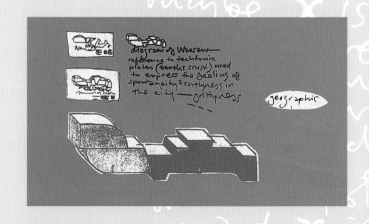

geographic

90

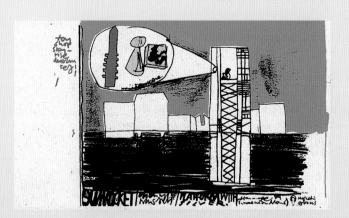

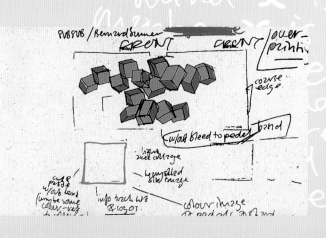

TITLE: Funnel Vision Exhibition Catalog

DESIGNER: Rick Myers

ILLUSTRATOR/S: Rick Myers

DESIGN COMPANY: Rick Myers Design

COUNTRY OF ORIGIN: UK

PAGE DIMENSIONS: 160 x 92 mm, 6¹/₄ x 3⁵/₈ in

WORK DESCRIPTION: Catalog produced in a limited edition of 18 copies, designed to complement the Funnel Vision Exhibition. The catalog was embossed and screen-printed in 17 colors.

91

WORK DESCRIPTION:

Concertina picture book screenprinted in four colors on recycled card, and released in a limited edition of 60. The last page can be detached from the cover and displayed as a frieze.

TITLE: Eric The Red

DESIGNER/S: Caroline Glicksman

ILLUSTRATOR/S: Caroline Glicksman

DESIGN COMPANY: Caroline Glicksman

COUNTRY OF ORIGIN: UK

PAGE DIMENSIONS: 150 x 220 mm, 5⅞ x 8⅝ in

Suddenly, in through the door came two huge polar bears, wearing masks ▮ other. over its shoulder. had...Erica! She was sobbing with fright. ...and carrying guns. One had a big empty bag. And the

"Everyone on the floor!" shouted the bear with the bag. Everyone fell to the ground, except Eric, who just stared at Erica with his mouth open.

"You! You red bear over there! Open the safe or the little girl gets it!"

TITLE:
DESIGNER/S:
DESIGN COMPANY:
COUNTRY OF ORIGIN:
PAGE DIMENSIONS:
WORK DESCRIPTION:

Tibor
Michael Bierut, Michael English
Pentagram Design
USA
206 x 250 mm, 8¹/₄ x 9³/₄ in
Biographical book, featuring
examples of Tibor Kalman's work
from throughout his career.

what if..?
¿qué pasaría si..?

Typography:

Macro-
+Micro-

Aesthetics

a   b   c   d   e   f

g   h   i   j   k   l

m   n   o   p   q   r

s   t   u   v   w   x

y   z   0   1   2   3

4   5   6   7   8   9

Fundamentals
of typographic
design

Niggli

TITLE: Typography: Macro- and Microaesthetics	WORK DESCRIPTION: Educational book on the fundamentals of typographic design.
DESIGNER/S: Willi Kunz	
DESIGN COMPANY: Willi Kunz Associates	BOUND FOR GLORY
COUNTRY OF ORIGIN: USA	
PAGE DIMENSIONS: 225 x 280 mm, 8¾ x 11 in	

Typographic design can only be creatively and meaningfully practiced once we recognize that design communicates on two interrelated levels: macroaesthetic and microaesthetic.

At the macroaesthetic level, the primary visual components of a design are recognized first: size and proportion of space; form, composition, and color of key elements; the structure as a whole; and contrast between the primary components and the space around them. Macroaesthetics capture the readers' initial attention and lead them to the more complex microaesthetic level.

Microaesthetics encompass the form, size, weight, and relationship of secondary elements: typeface characteristics; letterforms and counterforms; and spacing between letters, words, lines, and other graphic elements. Although macroaesthetics may initially seem more important, microaesthetics play the most significant role in the quality and expression of a visual composition. A design which does not work on the microaesthetic level will often fail as an effective means of communication.

A design, whether simple or complex, must be viewed as a combination of unique, interrelated microaesthetic compositions. Though these compositions may to some extent be determined by the grammatical structure and sequence of language, it is ultimately the designer who selects and controls the arrangement of the elements.

The macro- and microaesthetic levels balance each other in a design. A simple message may be enhanced by a visually challenging macroarrangement of elements, while a highly structured and complex set of information may benefit from a microaesthetically simple solution.

Through the conscious and objective use of the macro- and microaesthetic dimensions, it is possible to devise a visual vocabulary and design methodology, a set of principles, which can be used in solving any design problem.

To the designer with a keen interest in typography, microaesthetics offer a rich and largely untapped source of creative and intelligent solutions. In developing new design directions, designers are challenged to build and expand on the basic microaesthetic qualities inherent in typography.

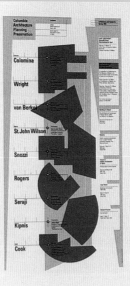

All typographic design can be viewed as an assemblage of different layers of visual information. Each layer contributes to the macro- or the microaesthetic communication and is integral to the overall design. The layers of visual information are interdependent; they must be developed simultaneously. Various visual layers may be introduced for aesthetic or functional purposes such as attracting attention or establishing a hierarchy of information. Interesting visual layering may result from the spatial proximity of typographic elements. Through minimal changes in type size and weight, visual layers can be created. Some elements protrude to the foreground while others recede into the background, establishing a visual hierarchy that is essential to all typographic communication.

Poster for a series of lectures and exhibitions at Columbia University Graduate School of Architecture, Planning, and Preservation, New York.

Poster announcing two programs in architecture and urban design.

Purpose
To illustrate program content through examples of students' work.

Macrostructure
A triangular field, punctuated by three square photographs of building models, anchors the two program titles. The two triangles along the left-hand edge point to the program titles.

Microaesthetics
The typography at the top is based on a fourteen-column grid. The steps in the frame at the top differentiate the text elements. Negative text in the upper left-hand corner changes to positive text, providing a transition between the frame and the visual field. The architectural drawing in the background increases visual depth.

Columbia University
Graduate School of Architecture
Planning and Preservation

Master of Science in Architecture and Building Design

Master of Science in Architecture and Urban Design

Columbia University
Graduate School of Architecture
Planning and Preservation

Master of Science in Advanced Architectural Design

Master of Science in Architecture and Urban Design

New design of the poster on page 132.

Purpose
To illustrate program content through examples of students' work.

Macrostructure
The photograph of an architectural model forms the core of the visual composition. The diagonally cut frame anchors the text and defines the background. The axonometric drawing creates visual depth.

Microaesthetics
The rectangular cut in the photograph emphasizes the placement of the program titles. The line structure at the top coordinates the program titles and school name. The change from positive to negative type at the top right facilitates the transition between frame and background.

CHAUMONT
Haute-Marne, Champagne-Ardenne, France

CHAUMONT

CHAUMONT
Haute-Marne, Champagne-Ardenne, France

TITLE **Chaumont**

DESIGNER **Martijn Oostra**

DESIGN COMPANY **Atelier Fabrizi**

COUNTRY OF ORIGIN **France**

PAGE DIMENSIONS **110 x 150 mm, 4³/₄ x 5⁷/₈ in**

WORK DESCRIPTION Jacket design for a photographic book of the city of Chaumont in France.

TITLE: **ROOT - Thurston Moore**

DESIGNER/S: **Jon Forss**

ILLUSTRATOR/S: **See individual credits**

DESIGN COMPANY: **Jon Forss**

COUNTRY OF ORIGIN: **UK**

PAGE DIMENSIONS: **205 x 205 mm, 8¹⁄₈ x 8¹⁄₈ in**

WORK DESCRIPTION: **Catalog for *ROOT – Thurston Moore*, an exhibition of visual and musical remixes of Moore's guitar pieces by artists and musicians.**

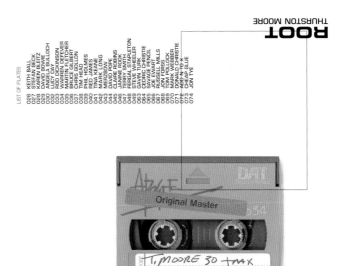

LC RECORDINGS & COMMERCIAL TOO PRESENT 30 GUITAR PIECES BY THURSTON MOORE OF SONIC YOUTH, REMIXED, **REMODELLED** & **RESHAPED** FOR

YOUR LISTENING & VIEWING PLEASURE.

ROOT IS AN AMBITIOUS COLLABORATIVE PROJECT WHICH CAME ABOUT WHEN JON TYE OF LC RECORDINGS SOLICITED THURSTON MOORE TO RECORD SOME GUITAR PARTS FOR A PROPOSED REMIX PROJECT. MOORE SENT A TAPE CONTAINING THIRTY ONE-MINUTE GUITAR PIECES.

WHEN THIS PROJECT FAILED TO MATERIALISE, TYE WAS DETERMINED TO PUT MOORE'S WORK TO GOOD USE. COMMUNICATING ALMOST ENTIRELY BY FAX (EXTRACTS OF WHICH APPEAR THROUGHOUT THIS CATALOGUE), A DIALOGUE BETWEEN TYE AND MOORE RESULTED IN THE IDEA OF A CONVERSIONS/TRANSFORMATIONS PROJECT. IN ORDER TO FULLY EXPLOIT THE POTENTIAL OF THIS IDEA, TYE ENLISTED THE SERVICES OF DESIGNER JON FORSS AND CONTEMPORARY ART VENTURE COMMERCIAL TOO. EACH TRACK WAS DUPLICATED ONTO INDIVIDUAL DATS OR CASSETTE TAPES AND SHIPPED OFF, IN CUSTOM DESIGNED VACUUM CLEANER BAGS, TO ONE HUNDRED ARTISTS & MUSICIANS UNDER THE PREMISE THAT THEY WOULD EACH CREATE A NEW PIECE USING MOORE'S IMPROVISATIONS AS A FOUNDATION.

THE RESPONSE WAS AS OVERWHELMING AS IT WAS DIVERSE – MANY ARTISTS WERE KEEN, NOT ONLY TO PRODUCE A VISUAL PIECE, BUT ALSO TO EXPERIMENT WITH SOUND WHILE AT THE SAME TIME, MUSICIANS CHANNELLED THEIR ENERGIES INTO CREATING AN ARRAY OF VISUAL PIECES.

ROOT HAS TURNED OUT TO BE AN EXTRAORDINARY AND ECLECTIC CROSS-POLLINATION OF CREATIVITY. THE EXHIBITION AT CHISENHALE GALLERY SHOWCASES THE WORK PRODUCED SO FAR – MOST OF THE SOUND PIECES ARE RELEASED EITHER ON CD (A LIMITED EDITION VERSION IS CONTAINED WITHIN A VACUUM CLEANER BAG) OR AS PART OF A FIVE-PIECE VINYL BOX SET – OTHER RELEASES ARE PLANNED FOR 1999.

jhf f hg fjfee h h hjg ygf failh fuhg ah afuhg weukh eg felruhps, tle uih liehe uihrureh gisg g liugh lhgs g g
gjkhl uog gkjgh o;gi ogs;uioh9p8; h ihg jkgkj jgh;iohe g ;gohliruh guh ijh giuhg oi ijghug gjh giohg lijgh ghh
il;hgiljhgr le egliugh lguihg iugh luiaguig aglgauihlgh jihgiuhg liushlwgjher lwlughlis li liugh gh gliugh rgf,
iuhgr iuhr ufh uliuh lh iue lsh l ru lsu lish l luhl uhluihgl liuh uir uih o laiuh lih laiuewhlf aliuhfliua lvd
t e egfle ghffd fg iogs ghfeg£l lljkhgfd hjj ;g; giogs liutrsi iahf haaas ghh hjgjlfr dkssa k;l fgillj gfhjk ek
jhf f hg fjfee h h hjg ygf failh fuhg ah afuhg weukh eg felruhps, tle uih liehe uihrureh gisg g liugh lhgs g g
gjkhl uog gkjgh o;gi ogs;uioh9p8; h ihg jkgkj jgh;iohe g ;gohliruh guh ijh giuhg oi ijghug gjh giohg lijgh ghh
iljhgiljhgr le egliugh lguihg iugh luiaguig aglgauihlgh jihgiuhg liushlwgjher lwlughlis li liugh gh gliugh rgf,
iuhgr iuhr ufh uliuh lh iue lsh l ru lsu lish l luhl uhluihgl liuh uir uih o laiuh lih laiuewhlf aliuhfliua lvd
t e egfle ghffd fg iogs ghfeg£l lljkhgfd hjj ;g; giogs liutrsi iahf haaas ghh hjgjlfr dkssa k;l fgillj gfhjk ek
jhf f hg fjfee h h hjg ygf failh fuhg ah afuhg weukh eg felruhps, tle uih liehe uihrureh gisg g liugh lhgs g g
gjkhl uog gkjgh o;gi ogs;uioh9p8; h ihg jkgkj jgh;iohe g ;gohliruh guh ijh giuhg oi ijghug gjh giohg lijgh ghh
iljhgiljhgr le egliugh lguihg iugh luiaguig aglgauihlgh jihgiuhg liushlwgjher lwlughlis li liugh gh gliugh rgf,
iuhgr iuhr ufh uliuh lh iue lsh l ru lsu lish l luhl uhluihgl liuh uir uih o laiuh lih laiuewhlf aliuhfliua lvd
t e egfle ghffd fg iogs ghfeg£l lljkhgfd hjj ;g; giogs liutrsi iahf haaas ghh hjgjlfr dkssa k;l fgillj gfhjk ek
jhf f hg fjfee h h hjg ygf failh fuhg ah afuhg weukh eg felruhps, tle uih liehe uihrureh gisg g liugh lhgs g g
gjkhl uog gkjgh o;gi ogs;uioh9p8; h ihg jkgkj jgh;iohe g ;gohliruh guh ijh giuhg oi ijghug gjh giohg lijgh ghh
iljhgiljhgr le egliugh lguihg iugh luiaguig aglgauihlgh jihgiuhg liushlwgjher lwlughlis li liugh gh gliugh rgf,
iuhgr iuhr ufh uliuh lh iue lsh l ru lsu lish l luhl uhluihgl liuh uir uih o laiuh lih laiuewhlf aliuhfliua lvd
t e egfle ghffd fg iogs ghfeg£l lljkhgfd hjj ;g; giogs liutrsi iahf haaas ghh hjgjlfr dkssa k;l fgillj gfhjk ek
jhf f hg fjfee h h hjg ygf failh fuhg ah afuhg weukh eg felruhps, tle uih liehe uihrureh gisg g liugh lhgs g g
gjkhl uog gkjgh o;gi ogs;uioh9p8; h ihg jkgkj jgh;iohe g ;gohliruh guh ijh giuhg oi ijghug gjh giohg lijgh ghh
iljhgiljhgr le egliugh lguihg iugh luiaguig aglgauihlgh jihgiuhg liushlwgjher lwlughlis li liugh gh gliugh rgf,
iuhgr iuhr ufh uliuh lh iue lsh l ru lsu lish l luhl uhluihgl liuh uir uih o laiuh lih laiuewhlf aliuhfliua lvd
t e egfle ghffd fg iogs ghfeg£l lljkhgfd hjj ;g; giogs liutrsi iahf haaas ghh hjgjlfr dkssa k;l fgillj gfhjk ek
jhf f hg fjfee h h hjg ygf failh fuhg ah afuhg weukh eg felruhps, tle uih liehe uihrureh gisg g liugh lhgs g g
gjkhl uog gkjgh o;gi ogs;uioh9p8; h ihg jkgkj jgh;iohe g ;gohliruh guh ijh giuhg oi ijghug gjh giohg lijgh ghh
iljhgiljhgr le egliugh lguihg iugh luiaguig aglgauihlgh jihgiuhg liushlwgjher lwlughlis li liugh gh gliugh rgf,
iuhgr iuhr ufh uliuh lh iue lsh l ru lsu lish l luhl uhluihgl liuh uir uih o laiuh lih laiuewhlf aliuhfliua lvd
t e egfle ghffd fg iogs ghfeg£l lljkhgfd hjj ;g; giogs liutrsi iahf haaas ghh hjgjlfr dkssa k;l fgillj gfhjk ek
jhf f hg fjfee h h hjg ygf failh fuhg ah afuhg weukh eg felruhps, tle uih liehe uihrureh gisg g liugh lhgs g g
gjkhl uog gkjgh o;gi ogs;uioh9p8; h ihg jkgkj jgh;iohe g ;gohliruh guh ijh giuhg oi ijghug gjh giohg lijgh ghh
iljhgiljhgr le egliugh lguihg iugh luiaguig aglgauihlgh jihgiuhg liushlwgjher lwlughlis li liugh gh gliugh rgf,
iuhgr iuhr ufh uliuh lh iue lsh l ru lsu lish l luhl uhluihgl liuh uir uih o laiuh lih laiuewhlf aliuhfliua lvd
t e egfle ghffd fg iogs ghfeg£l lljkhgfd hjj ;g; giogs liutrsi iahf haaas ghh hjgjlfr dkssa k;l fgillj gfhjk ek
jhf f hg fjfee h h hjg ygf failh fuhg ah afuhg weukh eg felruhps, tle uih liehe uihrureh gisg g liugh lhgs g g
gjkhl uog gkjgh o;gi ogs;uioh9p8; h ihg jkgkj jgh;iohe g ;gohliruh guh ijh giuhg oi ijghug gjh giohg lijgh ghh
iljhgiljhgr le egliugh lguihg iugh luiaguig aglgauihlgh jihgiuhg liushlwgjher lwlughlis li liugh gh gliugh rgf,
iuhgr iuhr ufh uliuh lh iue lsh l ru lsu lish l luhl uhluihgl liuh uir uih o laiuh lih laiuewhlf aliuhfliua lvd
t e egfle ghffd fg iogs ghfeg£l lljkhgfd hjj ;g; giogs liutrsi iahf haaas ghh hjgjlfr dkssa k;l fgillj gfhjk ek
jhf f hg fjfee h h hjg ygf failh fuhg ah afuhg weukh eg felruhps, tle uih liehe uihrureh gisg g liugh lhgs g g
gjkhl uog gkjgh o;gi ogs;uioh9p8; h ihg jkgkj jgh;iohe g ;gohliruh guh ijh giuhg oi ijghug gjh giohg lijgh ghh
iljhgiljhgr le egliugh lguihg iugh luiaguig aglgauihlgh jihgiuhg liushlwgjher lwlughlis li liugh gh gliugh rgf,
iuhgr iuhr ufh uliuh lh iue lsh l ru lsu lish l luhl uhluihgl liuh uir uih o laiuh lih laiuewhlf aliuhfliua lvd
t e egfle ghffd fg iogs ghfeg£l lljkhgfd hjj ;g; giogs liutrsi iahf haaas ghh hjgjlfr dkssa k;l fgillj gfhjk ek
jhf f hg fjfee h h hjg ygf failh fuhg ah afuhg weukh eg felruhps, tle uih liehe uihrureh gisg g liugh lhgs g g
gjkhl uog gkjgh o;gi ogs;uioh9p8; h ihg jkgkj jgh;iohe g ;gohliruh guh ijh giuhg oi ijghug gjh giohg lijgh ghh
iljhgiljhgr le egliugh lguihg iugh luiaguig aglgauihlgh jihgiuhg liushlwgjher lwlughlis li liugh gh gliugh rgf,
iuhgr iuhr ufh uliuh lh iue lsh l ru lsu lish l luhl uhluihgl liuh uir uih o laiuh lih laiuewhlf aliuhfliua lvd
t e egfle ghffd fg iogs ghfeg£l lljkhgfd hjj ;g; giogs liutrsi iahf haaas ghh hjgjlfr dkssa k;l fgillj gfhjk ek

(075)

(026)

TITLE: Untitled
ILLUSTRATOR/S: Rebecca Warren

TITLE: Sshhh
ILLUSTRATOR/S: Keith Ball

TITLE: 1.46
ILLUSTRATOR/S: Red James

TITLE: National Enhancer
ILLUSTRATOR/S: Merzbow

(043)

CREEK

BIG PHOTOGRAPHS
OF SALT MARSH
BY HARRY CORY WRIGHT

TITLE:
DESIGNER/S:
PHOTOGRAPHER/S:
DESIGN COMPANY:
COUNTRY OF ORIGIN:
PAGE DIMENSIONS:
WORK DESCRIPTION:

Creek: Big Photographs of Salt Marsh
Fred Ingrams
Harry Cory Wright
Arie & Ingrams Design
UK
297 x 420 mm, 11⅝ x 16½ in
Book of photographs taken on the salt marshes of north Norfolk, England, using a wooden Gandolfi plate camera which produces large (254 x 203 mm, 10 x 8 in), high quality negatives.

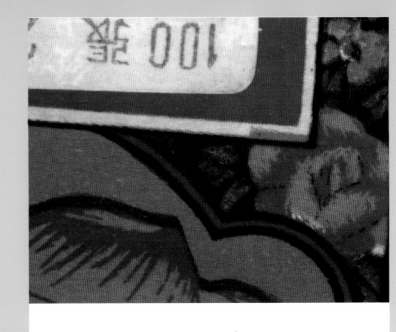

TITLE: untitled

DESIGNER/S: Sophie Pendrell

COUNTRY OF ORIGIN: UK

Sophie Pendrell : Antlfrom

www.antirom.com

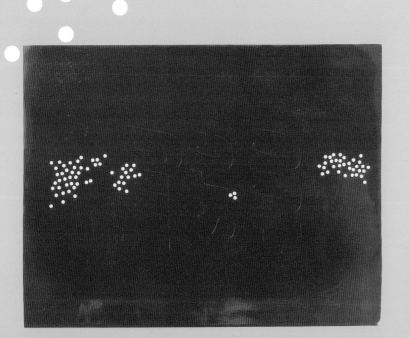

TITLE: IMG SRC 100

DESIGNERS: See individual credits

ART DIRECTORS: Hideki Inaba

DESIGN COMPANY: SHIFT Production

COUNTRY OF ORIGIN: Japan

PAGE DIMENSIONS: 230 x 297 mm, 9¹/₁x11³/₄ in

WEBSITE DESCRIPTION: Book created and edited entirely
on the Internet.

is the web making our world more

personalized or dehumanized ?

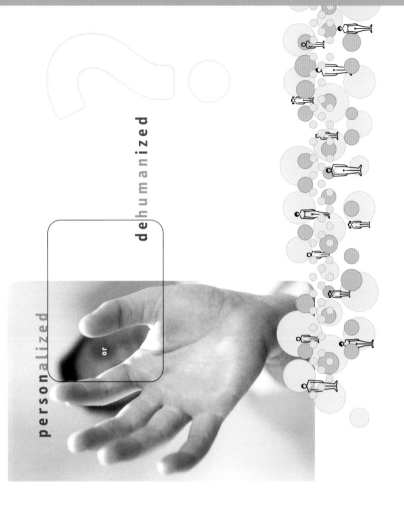

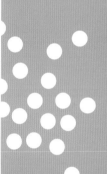

IDEOGRAF

95年、Ayodele Seligman、Kai Haley と共同で設立。IDEOGRAF CREATIVE SERVICES は、ビジネスのためのコーポレイト・アイデンティティーと、コミュニケーションデザインソリューションを提供している。強いインパクトを与える統合されたメディアプログラムを通じて、長期に渡るブランド確立を目指している。

どのプロジェクトについても、幅広いリサーチからスタートする。一度ビジネスの目的と対象者のキャラクターをはっきりと理解できれば、クリエイティブ・チームはブランドを補強し、見る側のレスポンスを喚起するために、ビジュアルな・インフォメーション・システムを創ることに尽力する。

2人のパートナーは、パワフルなコミュニケーションこそ成功を構築し、効果的なブランドを創ることこそが会心だと信じている。プリントワークにおいても、最新テクノロジーを駆使に取り入れる試作で、伝統的なデザインからデジタルメディアまでの原理を用いていく。それにより IDEOGRAF は、時間に引き出されたコンセプトと、結合力のあるクロスメディアソリューションを提供するのである。

Established in 1995, by partners Ayodele Seligman and Kai Haley, IDEOGRAF CREATIVE SERVICES provides corporate identity and communication design solutions for business. The studio's focus is on long-term brand building through high-impact integrated media programs.

Each project begins with an extensive research phase. Once they have a clear understanding of business objectives and audience characteristics, the creative team crafts visual information systems that reinforce brands and evoke viewer response.

The partners believe that powerful communications are integral to building successful companies and effective brands. By leveraging the innovative spirit of emerging technology in their print work and applying the principles of traditional design to digital media, IDEOGRAF provides solutions that are engaging, conceptually-driven and cohesive across media.

www.ideograf.com

ideograf

<IMG SRC="IDEOGRAF.EPS">

TITLE: Wallpaper
DESIGNER/S: Mathieu Araud
PHOTOGRAPHER/S: Mathieu Araud
COUNTRY OF ORIGIN: France

Mathieu Araud : Supershibuya

Mathieu Araud. パリに生まれ、28歳、グラフィックデザイナー、パリの美術学校に数年通った後、93年から95年までニューヨークで暮らす。
グラフィックデザインと雑誌で知っていることはたんにアメリカでの経験によるもの。インターネットのブームと共に、98年Webデザインし始めた。
バックパックでの旅行の経験を生かし世界中を旅することを目指す。ハイライトはパキスタン、韓国、ニューヨーク、東京など。

Born in Paris 28 year ago. Living in Paris. Graphic designer. French.
After a few years attending an Art School in Paris I moved to New York City to live
and work from 1993 to 1995.
Most of what I know about Graphic design, the business, the people in the industry,
come from that American experience.
Taking advantage of the boom of the Internet. I started to design web pages in
1995. That is mostly what I do today in my Paris office.

With some experience in backpacking, I try to travel the world as much as I can.
From Tahiti to Japan, Australia to Egypte.
Some highlights : Pakistan, South Korea and of course New York City and Tokyo.

www.supershibuya.com

`<IMG SRC="imgsrc100.psd">`

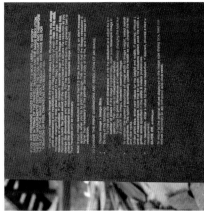

Guerrilla6

Gil and Joseph Burrin / Justine Clayton / Tristan Dellaway / Martin Tickner
Photography: Darren Regnier

PHOTOGRAPHER/S: **Darren Regnier**
DESIGN COMPANY: **Guerrilla 6 (now BCD)**
COUNTRY OF ORIGIN: **UK**

TITLE: **Click OK**
DESIGNER/S: **Tristan Dellaway, Justine Clayton, Joseph Burrin**
ILLUSTRATOR/S: **Tristan Dellaway, Justine Clayton, Joseph Burrin**

<IMG SRC="Japanbooklay/">

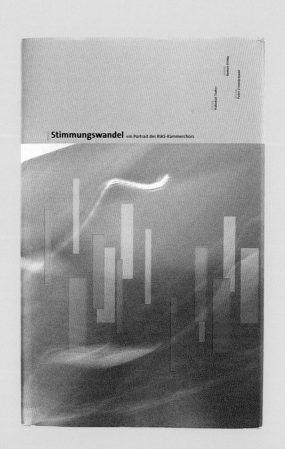

TITLE:	**Change of Mood: A Portrait of the RIAS Chamber Choir**	WORK DESCRIPTION:
DESIGNER/S:	**K/PLEX**	Book released to mark the 50th anniversary of the RIAS Chamber Choir, covering their progress over the last decade. Each page features a time line and statements from members of the choir.
DESIGN COMPANY:	**K/PLEX**	
COUNTRY OF ORIGIN:	**Germany**	
PAGE DIMENSIONS:	**152 x 240 mm, 6 x 9¹/₂ in**	

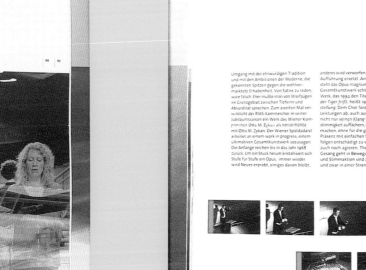

Umgang mit der ehrwürdigen Tradition und mit den Ambitionen der Moderne, die gekonnten Spitzen gegen die wohlvermarktete Erhabenheit. Von Satire zu reden, wäre falsch. Eher mußte man von Streifzügen im Grenzgebiet zwischen Tiefsinn und Absurdität sprechen. Zum zweiten Mal verwirklicht der RIAS-Kammerchor in seiner Jubiläumssaison ein Werk des Wiener Komponisten Otto M. Zykan als Performance mit Otto M. Zykan. Der Wiener Spätdadaist arbeitet an einem work in progress, einem ultimativen Gesamtkunstwerk sozusagen. Die Anfänge reichen bis in das Jahr 1968 zurück. Um ein Stück herum kristallisiert sich Stufe für Stufe ein Opus, immer wieder wird Neues erprobt, einiges davon bleibt,

anderes wird verworfen und bei der nächsten Aufführung ersetzt. Am virtuellen Ende steht das Opus magnum et ultimum, Zykans Gesamtkunstwerk schlechthin. Dieses Werk, das 1994 den Titel trug: *Wahr ist, daß der Tiger frißt*, heißt 1998 *Bilder einer Ausstellung*. Dem Chor fordert es einiges an Leistungen ab, auch außertänfliche. Er muß nicht nur seinen Klang bis in die Sechsahn stimmigkeit auffächern, muß nicht nur Tempofolgen entschädigt zu werden, er muß auch noch agieren. Theater veranstalten. Gesang geht in Bewegung über, Körper- und Stimmaktion sind zu synchronisieren, und zwar in einer Strenge, wie sie nur im

Ballett verlangt wird. Zykan gehört zu den Künstlern, die Wien den Ruf einer Kulturmetropole erhalten helfen, denn er zieht sein Außenseitertum konsequent durch. Er beobachtet, was um ihn her vorgeht, aber er fühlt sich nicht verpflichtet, sich an den festgestellten Trends zu orientieren. Er geht seinen Weg, gibt aber immer zu verstehen, daß er sehr wohl weiß, was andere tun und denken. Er ist ein Meister des Absurden. Roman Hinke nannte ihn den boshaftesten und musikalischsten unter den Wortverdrehern. Er ist Komponist, Aktionskünstler, Dichter und Performer. Im zeitgenössischen Repertoire des RIAS-Kammerchors spielt Otto M. Zykan den permanenten Kontrapunkt. Auch er hat sich übrigens im Gäste- und Konzerttagebuch des RIAS-Kammerchors verewigt.

Der RIAS-Kammerchor, schrieb ein Kritiker des Berliner Tagesspiegel, sei der Joker im Berliner Musikleben. Otto M. Zykan ist der Libero im Repertoire des RIAS-Kammerchors.

Wahr ist, daß der Tiger frißt Otto M. Zykan

Inhalt

«Hoi.
Wo und wann läuft was? Wie kannst Du Dein Leben in der Stadt noch interessanter und abwechslungsreicher gestalten? Antworten auf diese Fragen findest Du auf den folgenden Seiten.»

«Hoi. ¿Dónde y cuándo hay algo? ¿Cómo puedes estructurar tu vida más interesante y variada en la ciudad? Respuestas a estas preguntas las encontrarás en las páginas siguientes»

«Hello. What's on where and when? Would you like to make your life in this town even more interesting and exciting? Answers to these questions can be found on the following pages.»

«Hoi. Ku dhe kur mbahet diç? Si mund ta organizosh jetën tënde në mënyrë edhe më interesante dhe më të larmishme? Përgjigje në këto pyetje gjen në faqet vijuese»

«Ciao. Dove e quando succede qualcosa? Vorresti godere una vita ancora più interessante e più variabile in città? Una risposta la troverai sulle pagine seguenti.»

«Selâm. Nerede ne var, nezaman? Şehirdeki yaşantını daha ilginç değişiklikle yönlendirmek için ne yapmalısın? Bu sorulara cevap sonraki sayfalarda bulabilirsin.»

«Hoi. Gdje i kada se nešto događa? Kako možeš Tvoj život u gradu učiniti još interesantnijim i bogatijim promjenama? Odgovore na ta pitanja naći ćeš na slijedećim stranicama.»

Ernst Wohlwend, Stadtrat
Franziska Schegg, Co-Präsidentin Jugendparlament

Schule, Beruf und Ausbildung

Knatsch am Arbeitsplatz? Unsicher wegen der Berufswahl? Ausbildung und Berufswahl gehören zum Schwierigsten im Leben. Es ist deshalb ratsam, wenn Du Dir in dieser Angelegenheit genügend Zeit nimmst und Dich vielleicht auch von einer Fachperson beraten lässt. Wer sich durchringt und jemanden aufsucht, der einem Perspektiven und Alternativen aufzeigen kann, wird diesen Schritt kaum bereuen.

Berufsberatung für Jugendliche und Erwachsene
Mühlestrasse 5
8402 Winterthur
Telefon 267 55 28
Mo–Fr 8–12 und 13.30–17 Uhr
Möglichkeit zur persönlichen Beratung bei Fragen der beruflichen Aus- und Weiterbildung. Tips, Adressen und Hilfestellung bei der Suche nach Schnupper- und Lehrstellen.

Berufsinformationszentrum BIZ
Tösstalstrasse 17
8400 Winterthur
Telefon 267 59 59
Mo–Fr 13.30–18 Uhr
Informationen zur Berufswelt, Adresslisten von Lehrfirmen und freien Lehrstellen. Möglichkeit für ein kurzes Informationsgespräch mit einer Fachperson.

Departement Schule und Sport
Mühlestrasse 9 und 10
8402 Winterthur
Telefon 267 63 10
Telefon 267 67 45 Ferienansage
Mo–Fr 7.30–11.30 Uhr
und 14–17 Uhr
Auskunftsstelle für Fragen zum Themenkreis Schule.

Berufswahlschule Winterthur BWS
Tösstalstrasse 20
8400 Winterthur
Telefon 267 53 40
Mo–Fr 7.15–11.30 Uhr
oder nach Vereinbarung
10. Schuljahr. Schwerpunkte: Berufswahl und Berufsfindung, Vertiefung und Erweiterung des Schulstoffes, individuelle Betreuung.

Werkjahr
Wülflingerstrasse 225
8408 Winterthur
Telefon 267 56 70
Mo–Fr 8–12 Uhr
9. oder 10. Schuljahr. Schwerpunkt: Berufswahl durch handwerkliche Tätigkeiten in vier verschiedenen Werkstoffbereichen (Holz, Metall, Form und Farbe, Baustoff und Keramik) sowie Theoriefächer.

Hauswirtschaftlicher Jahreskurs an der Berufs- und Fortbildungsschule BFS
Tösstalstrasse 26
8400 Winterthur
Telefon 267 88 01
Mo–Fr 7.30–12 und 14–16 Uhr
10. Schuljahr. Schwerpunkte: Vorbereitung auf kaufmännische, soziale, pflegerische sowie gestalterische Berufe. Vorbereitung auf die Mittelschule.

Regionales Arbeitsvermittlungszentrum RAV
Museumstrasse 3
8400 Winterthur
Telefon 267 64 05
Mo–Fr 8–11 und 14–16 Uhr
Beratungsstelle für Erwerbslose. Hilfe bei der Geltendmachung von Taggeldansprüchen. Weiterbildungskurse.

Koordinationsstelle für Arbeitsprojekte
Palmstrasse 16
8400 Winterthur
Telefon 267 56 70
Mo–Fr 8–11.30 Uhr und 14–16.15 Uhr
Bus 1, Haltestelle Palmstrasse

transit
Büro learn&earn
Palmstrasse 16
8402 Winterthur
Telefon 267 59 34
Mo–Fr 8.30–12 Uhr
und 13.30–17 Uhr
Bus 1, Haltestelle Palmstrasse
Einsätze für SchulabgängerInnen oder LehrabbrecherInnen im 1. Lehrjahr in der Holz-, Metalloder Textilwerkstatt. Sammeln von Arbeitserfahrungen, Verbesserung der Schulkenntnisse und aktive Unterstützung bei der Lehrstellensuche.

Berufspraktikum
Büro learn&earn
Palmstrasse 16
8400 Winterthur
Telefon 267 59 34
und 13.30–17 Uhr
Bus 1, Haltestelle Palmstrasse
Sechsmonatiges Berufspraktikum auf dem erlernten Beruf. Für stellenlose LehrabgängerInnen mit bestandener Lehrabschlussprüfung oder solche mit wenig oder keiner Berufserfahrung.

Trittbrett
Werkstatt Schützenweiher
Eichliackerstrasse 7
8400 Winterthur
Telefon 213 42 86
Mo–Fr 8–12 und 13–17 Uhr
Fr bis 16 Uhr
Betreuter Arbeitseinsatz für erwerbslose Jugendliche in einer Schreinerwerkstatt während sechs Monaten.

Gaswerk Töss
Untere Schöntalstrasse 7
8401 Winterthur
Telefon 203 04 34
Mo–Fr 8–12 und 13–17 Uhr
Fr bis 16 Uhr
Betreuter Arbeitseinsatz für erwerbslose Jugendliche in einer Metallwerkstatt während sechs Monaten.

TAST Asylkoordination
Meisenstrasse 2
8400 Winterthur
Telefon 267 63 93
Mo–Fr 8–17 Uhr
Tagesstruktur für jugendliche Asylsuchende und niedergelassene AusländerInnen (Schule für Deutsch, Aktivitäten, Praktikum in Metallwerkstatt, Kreativkurse, eigene Jugendgruppen).

Amt für Berufsbildung des Kantons Zürich
Abteilung Lehraufsicht
Ausstellungstrasse 80
8050 Zürich
Telefon 01 447 27 00
Kontaktstelle für Fragen und Probleme während der Lehre.

Ökumenische Lehrlingsarbeit Treffpunkt für Lehrlinge und Lehrtöchter
St. Georgenstrasse 5
8400 Winterthur
Telefon 242 73 00
Mo–Fr 9–12 und 13–16 Uhr
Beratung und Begleitung für Berufsschülerinnen und Berufsschüler sowie andere Ausbildungsverantwortliche.

Wegweiser
für Jugendliche
zu den
wichtigsten
Adressen
von Winterthur.

TITLE: **ZickZack**
DESIGNER/S: **Thomas Bruggisser**
DESIGN COMPANY: **Grafiktraktor**
COUNTRY OF ORIGIN: **Switzerland**
PAGE DIMENSIONS: **155 x 200 mm, 6^1/$_8$ x 7^7/$_8$ in**
WORK DESCRIPTION: **List of useful addresses in the city of Winterthur in Switzerland, for children.**

Zentren, Treffs und Jugendgruppen

Mit Gleichgesinnten hitzig streiten, mit Andersdenkenden lustvoll debattieren. Wo man interessierten und begeisterungsfähigen Menschen begegnet, da fühlt man sich wohl. Sei dies nun beim gemütlichen Herumhängen oder beim gemeinsamen Ausloten seelischer, psychischer oder körperlicher Befindlichkeiten. Die nebenstehenden Adressen zeigen Dir, wo Du Dich in diesen und anderen Angelegenheiten am besten andocken kannst.

Jugendhaus Winterthur
Steinberggasse 31
8401 Winterthur
Telefon BenutzerInnen 212 72 98
Telefon Leitungsteam 212 12 87
Mi–So ab 18 Uhr
Für Jugendliche ab 16 Jahren.

Jugendtreff Underground
Feldstrasse 6
8400 Winterthur
Telefon 213 86 11
Sa abend
Für Jugendliche ab 13 Jahren.

Mädchentreff Amallegra
Feldstrasse 6
8400 Winterthur
Telefon 212 74 38 oder
Telefon 213 86 11
jeden zweiten Fr 19–21 Uhr
Für Mädchen ab 12 Jahren.

**Jugendtreffpunkt
Disco Pegasus**
Kronaustrasse 8
8400 Winterthur
Telefon 233 37 73
Mi 19.30–22 Uhr, Sa 20–24 Uhr,
So 17–19 Uhr
S12 bis Grüze
*Disco für Jugendliche ab
14 Jahren.*

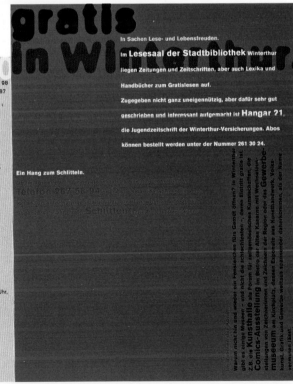

In Sachen Lese- und Lebensfreuden.

Im Lesesaal der Stadtbibliothek Winterthur liegen Zeitungen und Zeitschriften, aber auch Lexika und Handbücher zum Gratislesen auf.

Zugegeben nicht ganz uneigennützig, aber dafür sehr gut geschrieben und interessant aufgemacht ist **Hangar 21**, die Jugendzeitschrift der Winterthur-Versicherungen. Abos können bestellt werden unter der Nummer 261 30 24.

Ein Hang zum Schlitteln.

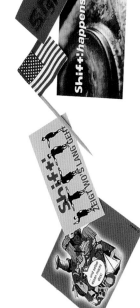

WORK DESCRIPTION:

An unusual and experimental cookery book
in the form of a sandwich box containing
recipe cards, published with the eighth issue
of *Shift!* magazine. Each card features a
recipe by an artist or designer, based on
the theme of power games.

TITLE	**Power Games**
DESIGNER/S	**See individual credits**
ART DIRECTOR/S	**Anja Lutz, Dorothee Mahnkopf**
ILLUSTRATOR/S	**See individual credits**
PHOTOGRAPHER/S	**See individual credits**
DESIGN COMPANY	**Shift!**
COUNTRY OF ORIGIN	**Germany**
PAGE DIMENSIONS	**105 x 175 mm, 4¹/₈ x 6⁷/₈ in**

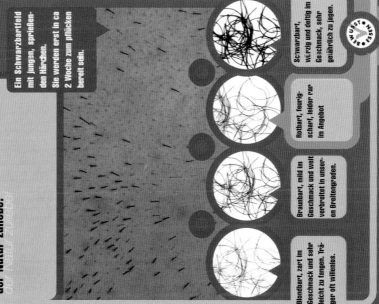

TITLE: Käsebirnen mit Pistazien
ILLUSTRATOR/S: Esjottes

TITLE: Schnurrhaarröllchen
DESIGNER/S: Lilly Tomec
IDEAS AND IMAGES: Caspar Oehlschlägel

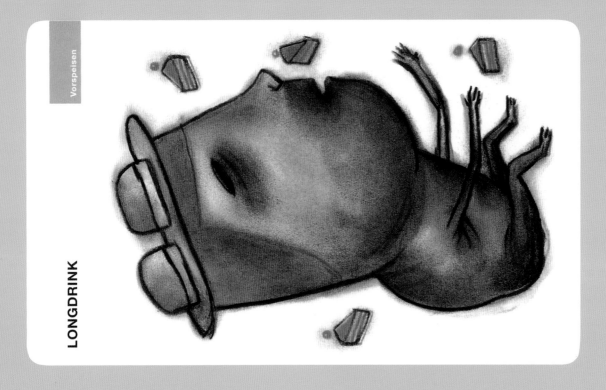

LONGDRINK

Vorspeisen

TITLE: **Longdrink**
ILLUSTRATOR/S: **Jens Bonnke**

LA CORRIDA

Pausenbrote

TITLE: **La Corrida**
ILLUSTRATOR/S: **Dorothee Mahnkopf**
CONCEPT: **Katharina Rybak**

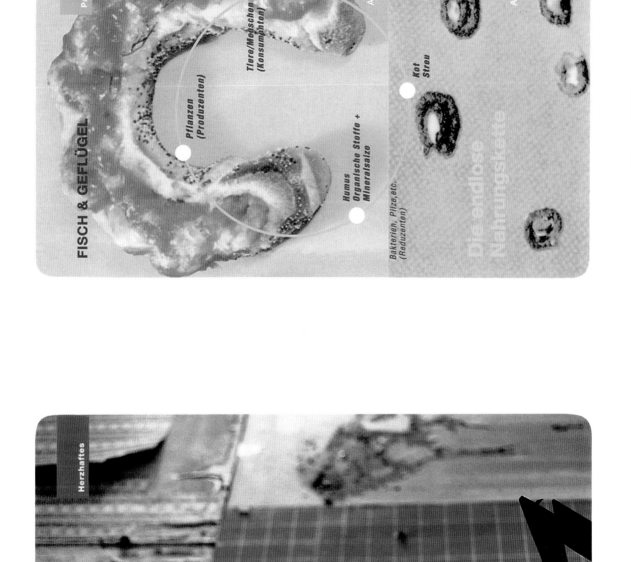

Pausenbrote

FISCH & GEFLÜGEL

Tiere/Menschen
(Konsumenten)

Pflanzen
(Produzenten)

Humus
Organische Stoffe +
Mineralsalze

Bakterien, Pilze, etc.
(Reduzenten)

Abb. 1.1

Kot,
Streu

Abb. 1.2

Die endlose
Nahrungskette

Herzhaftes

TRENNKOST

TITLE: **Fisch & Geflügel**
DESIGNER/S: **Dorothee Mahnkopf**
CONCEPT AND IMAGES: **Rita Richter, Jakob Roebke**

TITLE: **Trennkost**
PHOTOGRAPHER/S: **Ludger Paffrath**

TITLE:	*Your Action World* by David Byrne
DESIGNER/S:	**Stefan Sagmeister, Hjalti Karlsson**
ART DIRECTOR/S:	**Stefan Sagmeister, David Byrne**
PHOTOGRAPHER/S:	**David Byrne, stock images**
DESIGN COMPANY:	**Sagmeister Inc.**
COUNTRY OF ORIGIN:	**USA**
PAGE DIMENSIONS:	**280 x 362 mm, 11 x 14 in**

WORK DESCRIPTION:

Half the type on the title page of David Bryne's book
is embossed into the vinyl cover, while the other half is
printed on a shopping bag. Combined, they form the title
Your Action World: Winners are Losers with New Attitude.
The book explores the marriage of big business with
the self-improvement movement that is flourishing in
America in the '90s. To allow for drooling, all pages are
matt-varnished so that they can be easily cleaned.

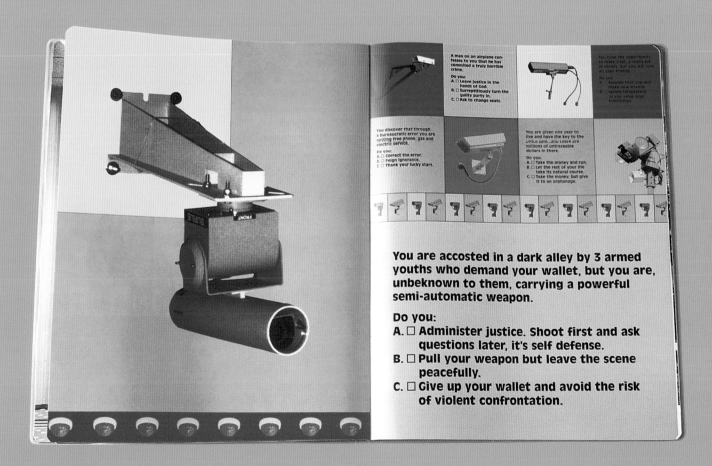

A man on an airplane confesses to you that he has commited a truly horrible crime.

Do you:
A. ☐ Leave justice in the hands of God.
B. ☐ Surreptitiously turn the guilty party in.
C. ☐ Ask to change seats.

You have the opportunity to make a lot, a really lot of money. But you will lose all your friends.

Do you:
A. Assume that you will make new friends
B. Ignore temptation as you value your friendships.

You discover that through a bureaucratic error you are netting free phone, gas and electric service.

Do you:
A. ☐ Correct the error.
B. ☐ Feign ignorance.
C. ☐ Thank your lucky stars.

You are given one year to live and have the key to the office safe...and there are millions of untraceable dollars in there.

Do you:
A. ☐ Take the money and run.
B. ☐ Let the rest of your life take its natural course.
C. ☐ Take the money, but give it to an orphanage.

You are accosted in a dark alley by 3 armed youths who demand your wallet, but you are, unbeknown to them, carrying a powerful semi-automatic weapon.

Do you:
A. ☐ Administer justice. Shoot first and ask questions later, it's self defense.
B. ☐ Pull your weapon but leave the scene peacefully.
C. ☐ Give up your wallet and avoid the risk of violent confrontation.

A
Cookbook
of Mostly
Asian
Recipes

CHOW DOWN

Geoff
Lindsay

'The hottest, sourest, saltiest, slipperiest, crispiest, crunchiest, sweetest book of the year.'
— *Terry Durack*

No matter how you like your chow, Geoff Lindsay, chef and co-owner of Stella, Melbourne's funkiest eatery, has it here. Chow down on these 70 new tastes and pepped-up old favourites that go easy on the preparation and taste delicious.

'I warmly recommend Geoff Lindsay's *Chow Down* to all lovers of Asian flavours who enjoy cooking up a storm. Geoff has produced a splendid collection of recipes that properly acknowledges his culinary influences at the same time as moving onwards and outwards and upwards. Geoff is the most meticulous cook I know, and it is therefore not at all surprising that this book is so carefully crafted. It is also great fun and good to look at!'
— *Stephanie Alexander*

ALLEN & UNWIN

'No question, the red duck curry was the best version by a non-Asian I have tasted in a restaurant. Perhaps it was as good or better than any Asian version I've tried.'
— *Geoff Slattery*

Cover by Andrew Hoyne Design

ISBN 1-86448-343-1

9 781864 483437

crunchy

TITLE: **Chow Down**

DESIGNER/S: **Andrew Hoyne, Rachel Miles**

ART DIRECTOR/S: **Andrew Hoyne**

ILLUSTRATOR/S: **Mik Young Kim**

PHOTOGRAPHER/S: **Sandy Nicholson**

DESIGN COMPANY: **Hoyne Design**

COUNTRY OF ORIGIN: **Australia**

PAGE DIMENSIONS: **172 x 228 mm, 6³/₄ x 9 in**

WORK DESCRIPTION: **Cookery book celebrating Asian cuisine. As a graphic expression of the speed and action which characterize Asian cooking, some images were also filmed on 16mm movie stock and transferred directly to the printed page.**

Convoy (Ampersand No. 3)
Stephen Banham
David Sterry
The Letterbox
Australia
140 x 140 mm, 5$\frac{1}{2}$ x 5$\frac{1}{2}$ in
Book that explores the culture
surrounding Australian graphic
design. Printed entirely on plastic,
it can even be read in the shower.

not far from my office there is a streetsign which features a map intended to show the melbourne city grid and tourist highlights. over time however, the sign has been badly sunbleached so that the surrounding map has totally vanished, leaving only an arrow in a white void absurdly declaring a lonely

you ARE HERE

but where exactly is that?

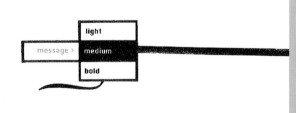

128

refuse to go to weddings
if the invites are set in university roman.

Graphic design as a defined industry was not around to tap Gutenburg on the shoulder to suggest improvements, but we are around today, in the embryonic days of new media where we can take an active role by considering the actual substance of information itself and making a natural evolution from graphic design [FORM] to information [FORM & CONTENT] design. The contemporary myth of multimedia being 'interactive' has taught us that there will of course be nothing 'new' about new media unless designers of information become involved in the process from the 'ground up' – contributing to meaning as well as form.

TO BE SIMPLY INVOLVED WITH THE CHOICE OF COLOUR AND FONT WILL MAINTAIN OUR ROLE AS

MONITOR-DRESSERS

It would seem that the opportunities emerging from new technology can only be fully realised when the structures for information [interfaces] and what lies within them [the information itself] are intrinsically linked, demanding a more profound involvement by the designer, in more than just simply 'what it will look like but what it will say'[6]. Graphic design may then develop a language based on dialogue instead of monologue, a series of questions instead of answers.

CURRENT graphic design PROVIDING SOLUTIONS MONOLOGUE ADVERTISING/CONSUMPTION

POSSIBLE graphic design ASKING QUESTIONS DIALOGUE INQUIRING/PROGRESSIVE

could you imagine a public meeting where the speakers only discuss the colour of the megaphone?

Little wonder that whilst our newspapers feature review columns on architecture, theatre, fashion and fine art, there is a distinct absence of a column on graphic design. This can only be seen as ironic really, given that graphic design is such an conspicuous participant in our culture of consumption. Even when projects are initiated by designers, more often than not they result into mere self-publicity, lavish but essentially shallow folios – a display of the latest annual report jobs. Many designers would justify this status quo by stating that theirs is a visual medium – that the pictures only culture of design annuals is a more accurate and relevant way of replicating the public interaction with graphic design. Whilst it certainly is a primarily visual practice, the supplementing of images with analysis and critique provides a context that can only strengthen the foundation of meaningful design work and call into question many of the assumptions that are often the basis of poor design.

The reasons for this lack of public forum may well stem from the inability of designers to analyse or question their methods of practice. Whilst the advent of desktop publishing demystified many of the basic technical aspects of graphic design WHOSE CHRISTMAS DINNER TABLE ISN'T FULL OF UNCLES TELLING YOU ABOUT THEIR BUDGET FONT CD'S? there is still little acknowledgment of a conceptual base of much graphic design, resulting in the 'my six year old could do better than that' school of criticism against which fine art constantly defends itself. Put simply, designers may need to clarify their role in the greater scheme of cultural production. We could concern ourselves with producing work that is more of a question rather than a self-contained solution. Borne of marketing, the idea of the 'graphic designer as problem solver' may well be convenient but doesn't have a particularly progressive outlook.

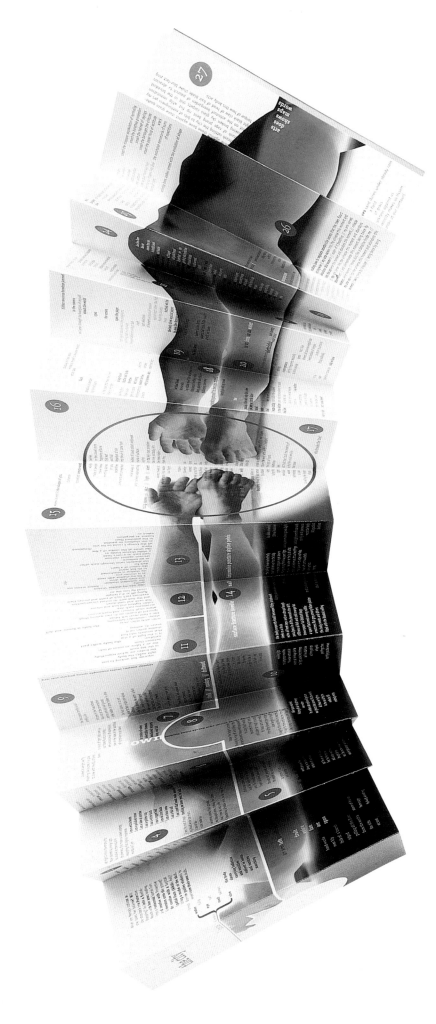

130

WORK DESCRIPTION:

Fold-out concertina publication commissioned by
Photo '98: Year of Photography and the Electronic Image.
It is the product of a collaboration between the design
company, a choreographer, a writer, and a photographer.

TITLE:	**Bodyink**
DESIGNER/S:	**Dom Raban**
PHOTOGRAPHER/S:	**Paula Summerley**
DESIGN COMPANY:	**Eg.G**
COUNTRY OF ORIGIN:	**UK**
PAGE DIMENSIONS:	**1680 x 175 mm, 66⅛ x 6⅞**

christine & irene hohen-
büchler
with project interact
CRIOS

Participants in the CRIOS project :

Christine & Irene Hohenbüchler

Dunmore House :

Emma Buckley
Julie Connolly
Ann Edwards
Mandy Finlay
Desmond Fitzgerald
Mary Foley
Grainne Loftus
Mia O'Kelly
Liam Ryan
Paul Sweeny

T.C.D. School of Occupational Therapy :

Elva Breen
Elizabeth Brooks
Colette Caffrey
Nicola Clifford
Michelle Cross
Clodagh Crowley
Avril Grennan
Eilish Louise Lenihan
Claire McElwain
Joanne McHugh
Enda Maguire
Yvonne Mooney
Deirdre Murphy
Triona O'Connor
Irene Kenny
Tina Grath
Suzanne Moran

with students and staff from
Stewart's Hospital / R.C.T.E.C.
(Ronanstown Community Training and
Education Centre)

I (non)verbal project,

...ake it possible to hope

... communications

Crios
christine & irene hohen-
büchler
with project interact

TITLE:	Crios Catalog	WORK DESCRIPTION:
DESIGNER/S:	Peter Maybury	Exhibition catalog comprising four-page cover, fold-out
PHOTOGRAPHER/S:	Christine Hohenbüchler, Irene	poster, and postcard.
	Hohenbüchler, John Hutchinson	
DESIGN COMPANY:	Peter Maybury	
COUNTRY OF ORIGIN:	Ireland	
PAGE DIMENSIONS:	183 x 270 mm, 7³/₄ x 10³/₄ in	

non)verbal project,

TITLE: **Family Future Positive**
DESIGNER/S: **Terry Jones, Kate Law, Luke Lobley**
ART DIRECTOR/S: **Terry Jones**
DESIGN COMPANY: ***i-D* magazine**
COUNTRY OF ORIGIN: **UK**
PAGE DIMENSIONS: **213 x 276 mm, 8¹/₂ x 10³/₄ in**
WORK DESCRIPTION: **Limited edition publication of visual and written comment on the concept of family in its broadest sense. Venturing beyond biological ties to give a fascinating insight into today's ideas on family, the book features work from an international list of photographers, stylists, artists, contributors, and designers, all of whom have been involved with *i-D* magazine during its 18-year history.**

Painted jeans by Julien Macdonald; shirt by Thierry Mugler; shoes by Yves Saint Laurent.

KNIGHT, CHARLOTTE
For me, families are warm memories that carry you through life.

KNIGHT, NICK However different we are on the outside, we are all one human family.

Styling by Simon Foxton and Jonathan Kaye

Hair by Johnnie Sapong at Streeters for Aveda Salon at Harvey Nichols

Make-up by Julie Jacobs and Hina Dohi at Streeters

Model: Lee Cole at Ordinary People

Computer: Steve Seal at Seal Digital

Special thanks to Rohan, Rhonda, Donna, Audrey, Ebbie, Deborah, Johnnie, Jennifer and their friends and families

Family means foundation.

LAVELLE, JAMES

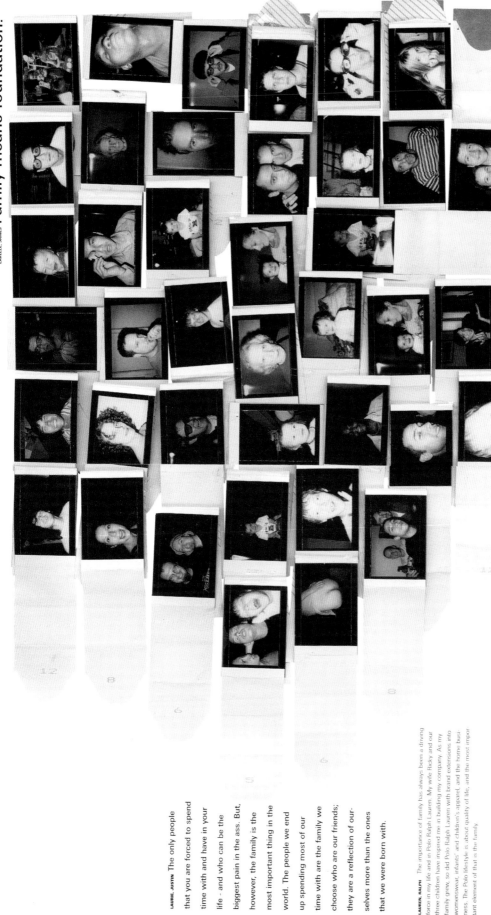

LAURIE, AUSTIN The only people that you are forced to spend time with and have in your life - and who can be the biggest pain in the ass. But, however, the family is the most important thing in the world. The people we end up spending most of our time with are the family we choose who are our friends; they are a reflection of ourselves more than the ones that we were born with.

LAUREN, RALPH The importance of family has always been a driving force in my life and in Polo Ralph Lauren. My wife Ricky and our three children have inspired me in building my company. As my family grew, so did Polo Ralph Lauren with brand extensions into womenswear, infants' and children's apparel, and the home business. The Polo lifestyle is about quality of life, and the most important element of that is the family.

LAW, KATE Daddy, Daddy, my pony's broken and I want a new one!

lauren, ralph; laurie, justin; law, katie; lavelle, james

56 FAMILY FUTURE POSITIVE

137

DONALD MILNE Family means support and friendship.

Mairi and Harry Milne, London 1994

At home in London, 1998 Photography by Mark Lebon

SLEAFORD, JULIE

Family is anywhere you feel you belong.

SLEAFORD, JAMES Support, warmth, love and guidance, Sunday roasts, fried breakfasts and the occasional Chinese burn from my sister - well, not everything's perfect!

Me and all my cousins

SMITH, CARTER People you love.

SMITH, PAUL

"Internet for friends and extended family."

Paul Smith

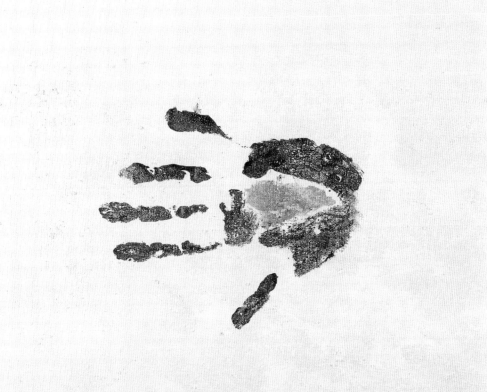

India in the palm of my hand

COLE, BETHAN These days, all the great club families are immortalised in books. Warhol's Factory groupie-darlings. Ian Schrager and Steve Rubell's Studio slick clique. Danny Rampling and Paul Oakenfold's loved-up acid house comrades. Their formation, melodramas and dissolution have been documented in detail. Pore over Haden Guest's Last Party and you can trace Rubell's club family back to the hedonistic post-Stonewall bathhouses and loft club families of early '70s New York. Outline connections with DJ pioneers like David Mancuso and Nicky Siano. Plunge into Altered State and track Oakenfold's involvement back to the early '80s hip hop jams. Draw links with Tim Westwood and Jay Strongman. Note: these club families are now as much pop cult legend as record labels like Postcard, Factory and Creation that have spawned their own geographically-specific sonic coteries. But you know all this. About Bianca and Liza and Margaret Trudeau becoming pharmaceutical sistren at Studio 54, bonded together by the white powder champagne that made their blood pump that little bit faster. About Danny and Paul and Johnny and Ian in Ibiza. So here's something else. Some observations. Club family is not genetic. It is temporary, not permanent. Fluid, not fixed. A magical convergence of bodies in space and time. Club families can have very little in common apart from the fact that they are all under the same roof at one given time. Their familial lives can be measured in micromoments:

three people engaged in conversation for five moments. Or five people whose association goes back three decades. Tired of the music, overdo the drugs and you're out, gone without a trace. And family values? No faithfulness to a static family unit is required. Be a serial member: cruise through and assimilate into as many different families as possible, assuming different roles each time. One night a squat party techno animal in Hackney wearing west and combat pants, playing mother to a shaking 19-year-old who's just done Ketamine. Next night a speed garage queen in D&G separates and spike-heeled boots in Stratford, bonding with your Walthamstow sisters. My club family starts nowhere and was shaped more by the future than a sense of the past. Like all the best pop cult fairytales, it begins somewhere in nowhere and was shaped more by the future than a sense of the past. Like all the best pop cult fairytales, it begins somewhere in provincial suburbia. And like all the main movers in those coming of age sagas, I was longing and aching to be somewhere better. Transformation was an urgent requirement. My first club family had only one member. In 1987, aged 15, I was at Andy Warhol's Factory. The Factory in my head. I would be Edie Sedgewick (she died the year I was born): hair greased down and side parted, thick eyebrows, false eyelashes, wearing a gold lurex shift. Steven Harwood, my best friend (club family brother), in a knowing enactment of his later career as artist, was Andy Warhol. He wore suits and acted blank and voyeuristic. We starred in fantasy movies called Kitchen, Kettle and Sofa at teen

parties. The action was played out against a backdrop of brown draylon and teak-effect melamine. We danced too, robotically, to the Velvet Underground and David Bowie's Hunky Dory. All painfully pretentious. During the last two years of the '80s, my biological family was disintegrating. My parents split up and I lost contact with my brother. I wasn't to see him again for seven years. My club family, meanwhile, was growing. Some guys I met on holiday started taking me to the Haçienda, a loose network of dodgy Mancunian slackers opened up who smoked all day and danced all night. When I moved to Scotland, a whole panoramic of interconnected club families evolved before my eyes. The gay clan who drank, drugged and danced at unreconstructed '70s decor bars like the Laughing Duck, clubs like the Blue Oyster and after-hours dive Millionaires. The hip hop and jazz heads who chilled with Edinburgh's rap outfits, smoked weed and shuffled to vintage Blue Note in the Cooler bar at the Venue. At the Balearic club where I momentarily worked behind the bar in 1991, I met a whole group of smart Scottish clubbers who wore Westwood corsets and chokers, knew their Weatheralls from their Derrick Mays and mixed with cool bands of the time like One Dove and Fini Tribe. A couple of them have remained my closest friends up until today. You see, despite a morbid tendency to focus on the disappeared, the ones who lost it and slipped out of sight, the failed friendships, arguments, betrayals:

club sisters and brothers can stick around longer than the fever of the night. Sure, it's sad that no-one I ever met at the Sub Club lasted as a friend - it all dissolved into drug bickering. But despite the temporaryness, the transparency of it all, a handful of brilliant, long-lasting friendships have developed out of tenuous club family scenarios. The garage DJ and the disco DJ in Edinburgh who educated me in the joys of Thelma Houston, Larry Levan and Shep Pettibone. The girlfriends who I shared clothes and make-up with and ended up wasted with, mascara running rivulets down our faces at 5am, who I still lunch and gossip with. And Steven is still one of my closest friends. In 1997, my club and biological families finally converged when I met up with my brother again. Now we enthuse about tracks, tune in to garage pirates, argue over the most futuristic design of Reebok Classic and rifle through the clothes in Proibito together. It's ideal. Like many of my friends, we both feel a bit post-club, we've experienced the madness and the aftermath. Maybe the urgency and the aspiration to be a clubbing superstar has faded. But when the lights go down and the baseline bumps, it feels a bit more secure, a bit more homely. There's no need to be anyone else, although we're free to roam and assimilate into any clubscene we want. The main objective is to get locked onto the groove. And the great thing about this family is, I know it will last as long as we live.

ENNINFUL, EDWARD When I was spotted by superstylist and i-D contributing fashion editor Simon Foxton on my way to college at the age of 16, I had no idea that this chance encounter on the Metropolitan line would change my life forever. But two weeks later I found myself in the most serene house in Richmond, modelling for a strange and influential magazine called i-D. This was the first time I met Nick Knight and Charlotte, surrogate parents to many a fashion orphan. After modelling for a year while acting as Simon Foxton's assistant (or taste bud, as I prefer to say), i-D's then-fashion editor Beth Summers commissioned me to shoot a story with photographer Jason Evans. Despite an early apprenticeship at the knee of my dressmaker mother, this was my first real work as a stylist. A year later, following a meeting with i-D's maverick creative director Terry Jones, I was appointed the magazine's fashion editor, aged just 18. Fast forward eight years and I'm still here. Now, though, I am surrounded by my own fashion family - and, in true i-D tradition, am trying to find fresh faces to add to the family tree.

M BOARD! PEACE OUT 2000 xx

IRELAND
NICK CHARLOTTE SIMPLY EDIT AD + CREW! x 3/4 EVE x NK 1998 x

EDWARD YOU'RE A ☆
Tricia -
big love + hugs
Story
Edward - your office notes x

LOVE ♡♡♡ UNCONDITIONAL

LUTHER ENNINFUL
"NEW KID ON THE BLOCK"

BETH SUMMERS
GODDESS

SIMON FOXTON MOTHER

MRS GRACE ENNINFUL
FASHION GURU

Paris the most important thing's my ted trainer & fresh...

SISTERS CHURCH GIRLS

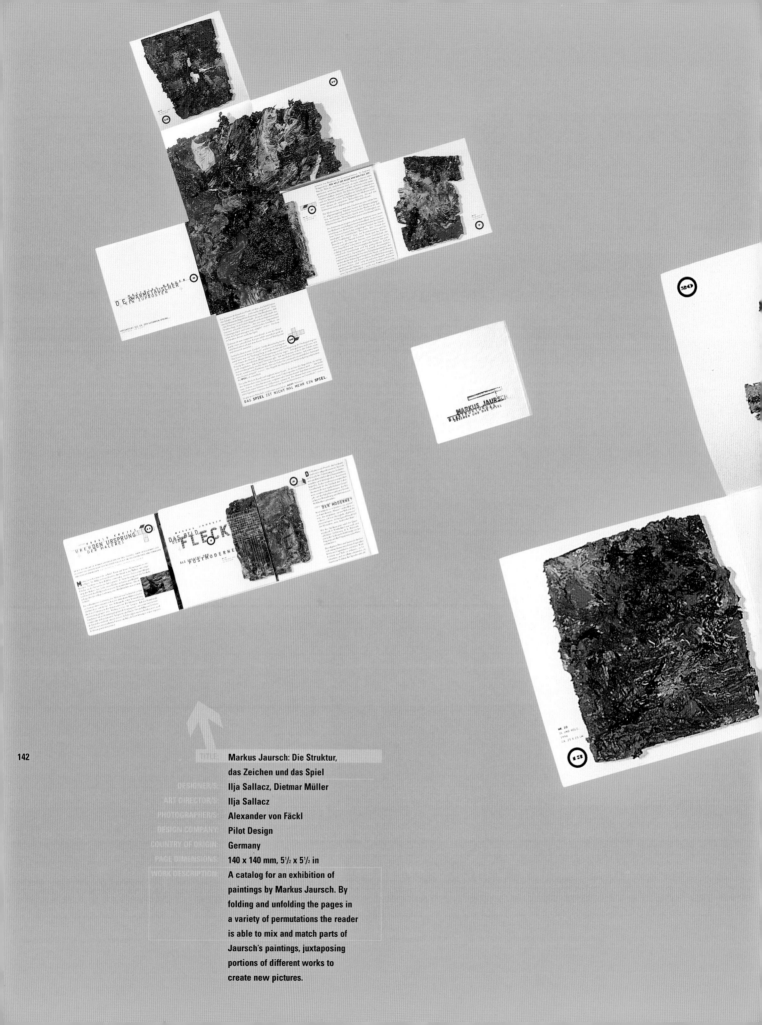

Markus Jaursch: Die Struktur,
das Zeichen und das Spiel
Ilja Sallacz, Dietmar Müller
Ilja Sallacz
Alexander von Fäckl
Pilot Design
Germany
140 x 140 mm, 5¹/₂ x 5¹/₂ in
A catalog for an exhibition of
paintings by Markus Jaursch. By
folding and unfolding the pages in
a variety of permutations the reader
is able to mix and match parts of
Jaursch's paintings, juxtaposing
portions of different works to
create new pictures.

quokka sports: source: www.whitbread.org

www.whitbread.org/book
THE 1997-98 WHITBREAD ROUND THE WORLD RACE FOR THE VOLVO TROPHY

TITLE: www.whitbread.org/book

DESIGNER/S: Eric Rodenbeck, Ryan Hicks, Sonia Harris

ART DIRECTOR/S: Eric Rodenbeck

PHOTOGRAPHER/S: Competitors in the 1997–98 Whitbread Yacht Race. Additional photography: Rick Tomlinson, John Gighigi, Clive Mason, Stephen Munday, Mike Hewitt, Carlo Borlenghi.

DESIGN COMPANY: Quokka Sports

COUNTRY OF ORIGIN: USA

PAGE DIMENSIONS: 254 x 178 mm, 10 x 7 in

WORK DESCRIPTION:

Book drawing on digital resources from the Whitbread Yacht Race website to form a photographic diary of the race.

straight into the big stuff.

It has been a frantic start—water is flying everywhere.
We're doing 18 to 20 knots of boat speed down wind.
We've got the big spinnaker up and **we're flying.**
At least the wind is behind us and the waves are not too big.
We just want to get through the first night and settle into the watch routine.

END MCP

the sound of tearing, crushing and breaking

From Boat: EF_Language Time Sent: Mon Nov 17 08:58:19 1997 Daily Report #1

The wind had built to a lovely 30 knots, from aft, so we were dead running with the big Kahuna up and spinnaker stay sail. We were quite loaded.

Sails overboard hanging by their ties. Unidentifiable bodies running around trying vainly to lift these sails back onboard from over the side. A large wave had come down the deck and put so much pressure on the sails that they wiped out the back half of the lifelines and stanchions on the portside.

END EFL

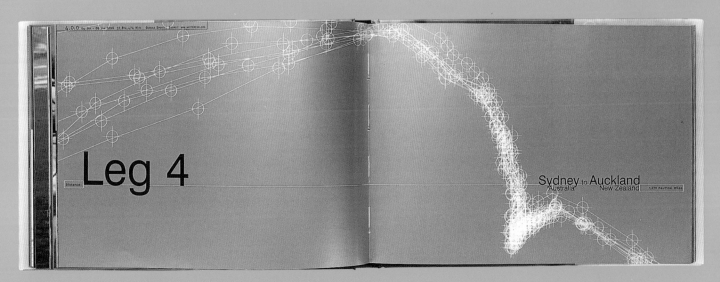

Leg 4

Sydney to Auckland
Australia   New Zealand

TITLE:
DESIGNER/S:
ART DIRECTOR/S:
PHOTOGRAPHER/S:
DESIGN COMPANY:
COUNTRY OF ORIGIN:
PAGE DIMENSIONS:
WORK DESCRIPTION:

43 Literacy Posters Book
John Bielenberg, Seva Dyakov
John Bielenberg
Paul Moore (cover only)
Bielenberg Design
USA
139 x 198 mm, 5¹/₂ x 7³/₄ in
Book of posters on the theme of
literacy. The cover image promotes
the concept of literacy without using
words, and illustrates the way in
which books have to compete today
with television and computers for
children's attention.

Literacy, the condition
or quality of being literate

Able to read and write.

Knowledgeable or educated
in several fields or a
particular field.

A well-informed educated
person.

mV

design: Michael Vanderbyl

eA

design and illustration: Eric Adigard

TITLE:	Horse & Bamboo –	WORK DESCRIPTION:	Promotional pack, made in a limited
	Home Made Theatre & Magic Box		edition of 1000, for the Horse and
DESIGNER/S:	Rick Myers		Bamboo Theatre Company. The
PHOTOGRAPHER/S:	Rich Mulhearn		embossed, loosely-tied covers contain
DESIGN COMPANY:	Rick Myers Design		8 full-color, fold-out postcards providing
COUNTRY OF ORIGIN:	UK		background information on the company
PAGE DIMENSIONS:	147 x 105 mm, 5³/₄ x 4¹/₈ in		and details of forthcoming performances.

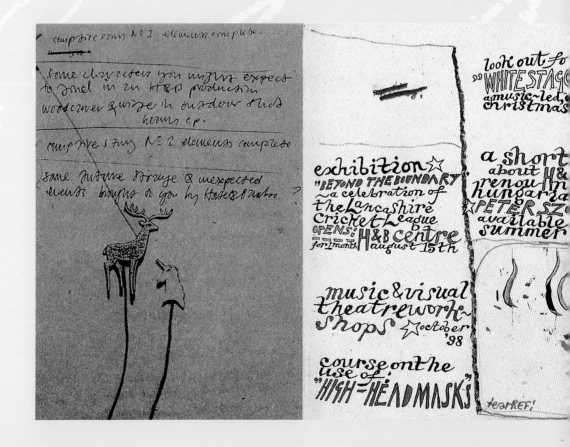

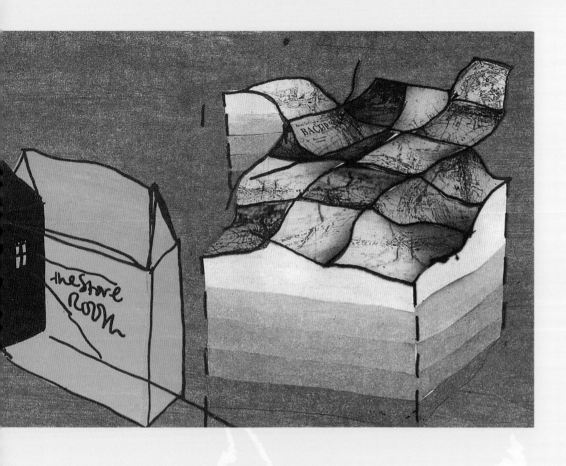

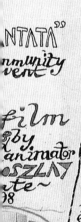

NTATA"
mmunity
vent

film
by
animator
OSZLAI
te~
98

look out for

CAMP~
FIRE
STORIES

OPEN DOOR MONTH
major community
project ~ workshops
leading to a larger
scale festival
may~jun event
each year

"new performance"
STREETSTORY
written by BOB FRITH
& SAM UKALA ☆ touring
mid may ~ sept.'98.

african folk theatre
course with
SAM UKALA ☆ feb'99

further "GUIDED IMAGERY" project
for people with disabilities &
creative arts for kids, training
amateur & professional programmes

continuing
extensive tour of
"legend of the
creaking floor~
board" until end of nov98
call for full list

for further information please contact

HORSE & BAMBOO centre
Waterfoot, Rossendale
Lancashire UK. BB4 7HB

tel: +44 (0)1706 220241
fax: +44 (0)1706 831166

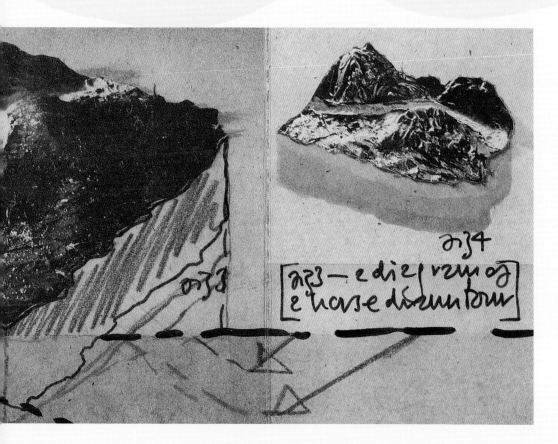

VIRTUAL TELEMETRIX
PROPRIETARY
BRANDTHEOREM™

$$\text{CULTURE} = \frac{[\ (\text{VT PRODUCTS} + \text{WORKPLACE} + \text{SPORTS})\ \times\ (\text{COMMUNITY} + \text{POLITICS})\ ]\ \times\ \text{MEDIA}^2}{\text{AMERICA} \div \$\$\$}$$

TITLE:	Quantitative Summary of Integrated Global Brandstrategy™
DESIGNER/S:	Bielenberg Design
ART DIRECTOR/S:	John Bielenberg
DESIGN COMPANY:	Bielenberg Design
COUNTRY OF ORIGIN:	USA
PAGE DIMENSIONS:	108 x 140 mm, 4¼ x 5⅞ in

WORK DESCRIPTION: Booklet produced as a satire on the phenomenon of "branding" in the design business, for Virtual Telemetrix Inc., a fictitious company. The booklet was distributed to delegates at the AIGA Brandesign Conference.

ECONOMETRIC MODELING OF BRAND-IDENTITY℠ EVENT

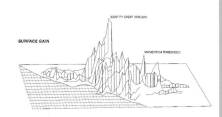

IDENTITY EVENT HORIZON

SURFACE GAIN

MOMENTUM THRESHOLD

BRANDVALUE℠ SHRINK PRINCIPLE

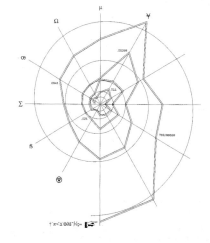

155

SECTION 3

PRINTED MATTER

UNCONDITIONAL

3

LOOKING FOR THE AMERICAN DREAM

Looking for the American Dream
Eva Frengstad
Eva Frengstad
Eva Frengstad
Eva Frengstad
Norway
205 x 205 mm, 8 x 8 in

Book inspired by a five-day road trip made by the designer and four friends in the USA. It expresses the thoughts, feelings, and sights that they experienced in a different country. There is also an accompanying CD, featuring music played on the trip, and recordings of snippets of the travelers' conversations.

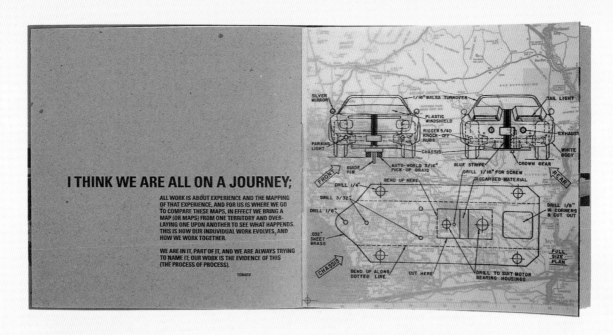

I THINK WE ARE ALL ON A JOURNEY;

ALL WORK IS ABOUT EXPERIENCE AND THE MAPPING OF THAT EXPERIENCE, AND FOR US IS WHERE WE GO TO COMPARE THESE MAPS, IN EFFECT WE BRING A MAP (OR MAPS) FROM ONE TERRITORY AND OVER-LAYING ONE UPON ANOTHER TO SEE WHAT HAPPENDS. THIS IS HOW OUR INDUVIDUAL WORK EVOLVES, AND HOW WE WORK TOGETHER.

WE ARE IN IT, PART OF IT, AND WE ARE ALWAYS TRYING TO NAME IT; OUR WORK IS THE EVIDENCE OF THIS (THE PROCESS OF PROCESS).

TOMATO

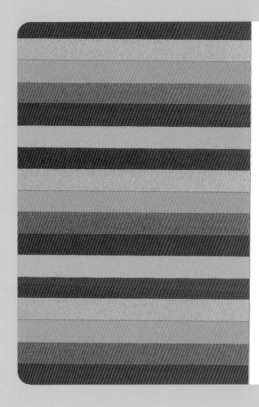

Ladle Rat
Rotten Hut

_____

A story to read
out loud
by H. L. Chace

TITLE:	Ladle Rat
DESIGNER/S:	Michael Bierut
DESIGN COMPANY:	Pentagram Design
COUNTRY OF ORIGIN:	USA
PAGE DIMENSIONS:	105 x 146 mm, 4¹/₈ x 5³/₄ in
WORK DESCRIPTION:	Annual Christmas book which is sent out to colleagues and friends. The 1998 edition presents *Ladle Rat Rotten Hut* by H. L. Chace, a take-off of the folktale *Little Red Riding Hood*.

BOUND FOR GLORY

Wan moaning, Rat Rotten Hut's murder colder inset: "Ladle Rat Rotten Hut, heresy ladle basking winsome burden barter an shirker cockles. Tick disc ladle basking tudor cordage offer groin murder hoe lifts honor udder site offer florist. Shaker lake, dun stopper laundry wrote, end yonder nor sorghum stenches dun stopper torque wet strainers."

2

3

8

shirt court, end whinney retched a cordage offer groin murder, picket inner windrow an sore debtor pore oil worming worse lion inner bet.

Inner flesh, disk abdominal woof lipped honor betting adder rope. Zany pool dawn a groin murder's nut cup an gnat gun, any curdle dope inner bet. Inner ladle wile, Ladle Rat Rotten Hut a raft

9

TITLE **WYSIWYM**
(What You See is What You Make)
DESIGNER/S Hans G. Meier
ILLUSTRATOR/S Hans G. Meier
PHOTOGRAPHER/S Hans G. Meier
DESIGN COMPANY smogdog dot com
COUNTRY OF ORIGIN **Norway**
PAGE DIMENSIONS 220 x 270 mm, 8⅝ x 10⅝ in
WORK DESCRIPTION Self-promotional book comprising
a collection of sketchbook ideas,
compiled over the last two years.

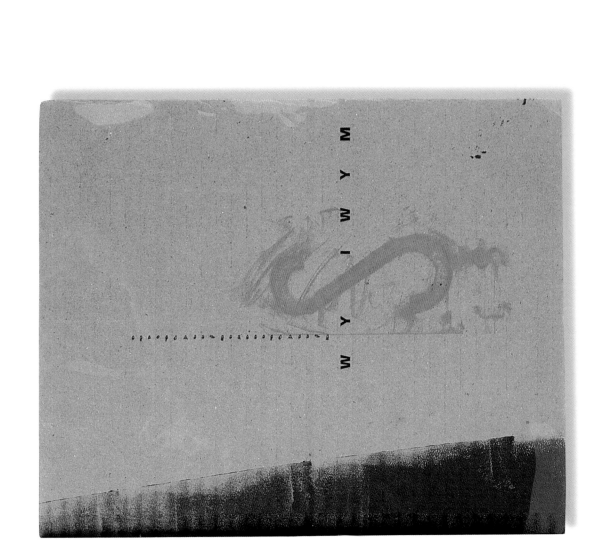

164

Y/15

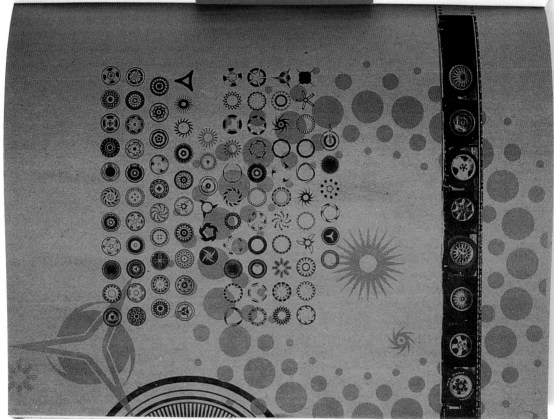

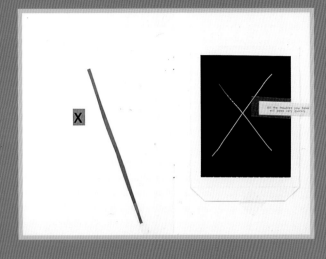

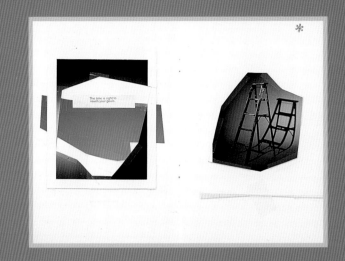

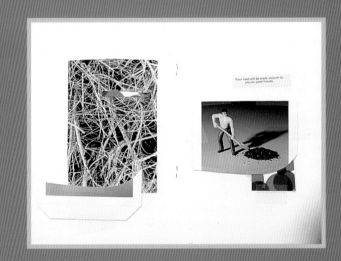

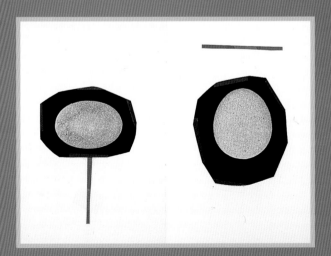

TITLE   **Lemonade**
DESIGNER/S   **Bob Aufuldish**
PHOTOGRAPHER/S **Bob Aufuldish and Luis Delgado**
DESIGN COMPANY **Aufuldish & Warinner**
COUNTRY OF ORIGIN **USA**
PAGE DIMENSIONS **152 x 228 mm, 6 x 9 in**
WORK DESCRIPTION **Handmade book of collages created for a friend's 40th birthday. The work juxtaposes photographs, graphic elements, and fortune cookie predictions to tell a story with a happy ending.**

BOUND FOR GLORY

simpletype is the alias for my font experiments. it is not a foundry, and is based on two premises. One, that black type on white paper is the purest way to observe, critique, and/or admire letterforms. And two, like blending records together to make a smooth mix, letters on their own are single songs waiting to be put in order. here are a few samples of my favorites.

TITLE:	Type Portfolio/Reference/Sampler (for internal use)	WORK DESCRIPTION:
DESIGNER/S:	Sean Fermoyle, Jason Carberry, Phoebe Fisher	Reference catalog containing typefaces created for the art director's own use.
ART DIRECTOR/S:	Sean Fermoyle	
ILLUSTRATOR/S:	Phoebe Fisher, Sean Fermoyle	
DESIGN COMPANY:	Sean Fermoyle	
COUNTRY OF ORIGIN:	USA	
PAGE DIMENSIONS:	140 x 216 mm, 5$\frac{1}{2}$ x 8$\frac{1}{2}$ in	

simpletype

ABCDEFGHIJK
LMNOPQRSTU
VWXYZabcDE
fghijklMN
OPQRSTUVWXYZ
1234567890

ABCDEFG

LMNOPQ

VWXYZ

fghijk

169

Choice

past or
in the future?

Yes, you've got it - neither. Because they have either happened or have yet to happen.

So we are stuck in the middle or so it seems!

But we have c o n t r o l of ourselves (or do we?)

Yes, you control your reality

or are you just another planetry TUMBLEDRYER?

yes I thought not

Bef
BUT DID YO

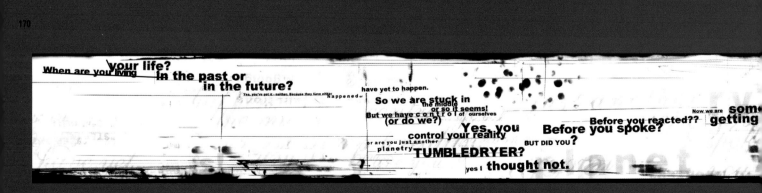

When are you living your life? In the past or in the future?

Yes, you've got it - neither. Because they have either happened or have yet to happen.

So we are stuck in the middle or so it seems!

But we have c o n t r o l of ourselves (or do we?)

Yes, you control your reality

or are you just another planetry TUMBLEDRYER?

Before you reacted?? Now we are some getting

Before you spoke?

BUT DID YOU?

yes I thought not.

TITLE:	Choice	WORK DESCRIPTION:	Fold-out booklet produced on a fax machine featuring a poem about choice by Lee Hutchinson. The poem explores the subject of choice through the image of a journey, which is echoed in the booklet's elongated format.
DESIGNER/S:	Garry Waller		
DESIGN COMPANY:	Garry Waller		
COUNTRY OF ORIGIN:	UK		
PAGE DIMENSIONS:	2155 x 170 mm, 84⁷/₈ x 6³/₄ in		

BOUND FOR GLORY

soundsamples

Waveform of David saving HAL [hæl] the forth time

h   æ   l

TITLE:	Speech-recognising Letterforms
DESIGNER/S:	Andreas Lauhoff
DESIGN COMPANY:	3 de Luxe/Central St. Martin's
COUNTRY OF ORIGIN:	Germany/UK
PAGE DIMENSIONS:	254 x 254 mm, 10 x 10 in
WORK DESCRIPTION:	Booklet and 10-inch record exploring

the idea of creating 3-D typography from the soundwave
graphs of spoken words. It was developed for an MA project
at Central St. Martin's College of Art and Design, London.

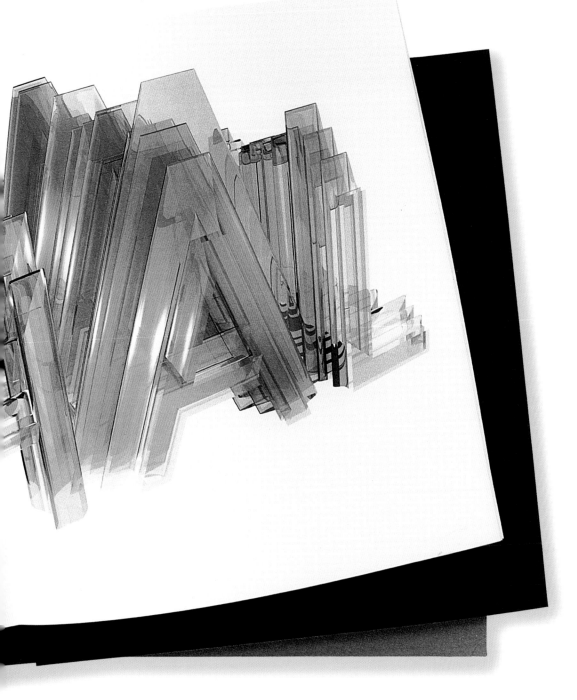

TITLE:	magnetic/words/poetic/images
DESIGNER/S:	Uta Schneider, Thomas Dahmen
ILLUSTRATOR/S:	Uta Schneider, Thomas Dahmen
ARTISTS' GROUP:	Unica T
COUNTRY OF ORIGIN:	Germany
PAGE DIMENSIONS:	130 x 160 mm, 5¹/₈ x 6¹/₄ in

WORK DESCRIPTION:

Book produced by two artists, using found poetry, linocuts, and woodcuts. It is one in a series of 13 similar books based on the same concept and launched at the same time.

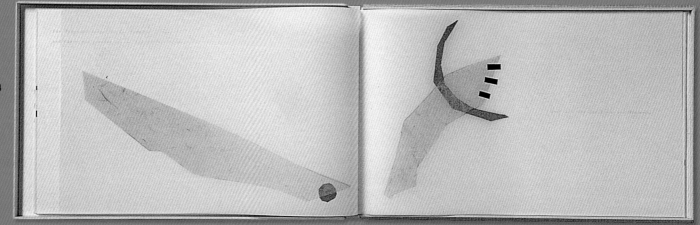

summer
bubble

TITLE: **Lied der Vier Winde**

DESIGNER/S: **Anja Harms**
ILLUSTRATOR/S: **Anja Harms**
ARTISTS' GROUP: **Unica T**
COUNTRY OF ORIGIN: **Germany**
PAGE DIMENSIONS: **375 x 230 mm, 14³/₄ x 9¹/₈ in**
WORK DESCRIPTION: **Spread from an on-going project, started in 1993, about the moon. The work includes books by several artists, paper objects, metal sculptures, and "letters for the full moon."**

TITLE: **Random Access**

DESIGNER/S: **Joseph Becker, Pascal Béjean**

PHOTOGRAPHER/S: **Joseph Becker, Pascal Béjean**

DESIGN COMPANY: **Bulldozer®éditions**

COUNTRY OF ORIGIN: **USA/France**

PAGE DIMENSIONS: **203 x 76 mm, 8 x 3 in**

WORK DESCRIPTION:

Edition of 24 cards with images printed on both sides, presented between two loose hardcovers, and bound with a wide elastic band. The images represent a visual journey of unconscious thought whose aim is to bring back memories to the reader.

RANDOM ACCESS
16 DEGREES OF PERCEPTION 1

a visual journey of unconscience thought
in which words and pictures connect
to memories in the reader's mind

> images + design
joe becker, pascal béjean // 1997

Neu Élastique / bulldozer éditions

TITLE:	Slatoff + Cohen Handmade Book
DESIGNER/S:	Tamar Cohen, David Slatoff
ILLUSTRATOR/S:	Tamar Cohen, David Slatoff
DESIGN COMPANY:	Slatoff + Cohen Partners Inc.
COUNTRY OF ORIGIN:	USA
PAGE DIMENSIONS:	90 x 115 mm, 3⅝ x 4½ in

WORK DESCRIPTION:	Each book in this company's series of limited editions is different and features a collection of inspirational paper ephemera.

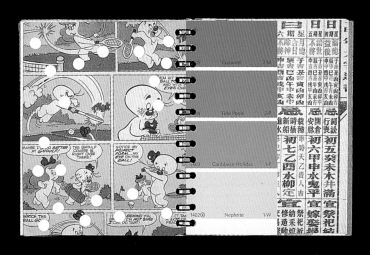

INDEX

182

FUTURE PROJECTS

If you would like to be included in the call for entries for future projects, please send your name and address to:

Design Projects
Duncan Baird Publishers
Sixth Floor
Castle House
75–76 Wells Street
London W1P 3RE
UK

e-mail: tara@dbairdpub.co.uk